16.⁰⁰

D0671805

A
BLOCKADED
FAMILY

A
BLOCKADED
FAMILY

By
PARTHENIA A. HAGUE

The Black Heritage Library Collection

 BOOKS FOR LIBRARIES PRESS
FREEPORT, NEW YORK
1971

First Published 1888
Reprinted 1971

Reprinted from a copy in the
Fisk University Library Negro Collection

INTERNATIONAL STANDARD BOOK NUMBER:
0-8369-8809-4

LIBRARY OF CONGRESS CATALOG CARD NUMBER:
78-157371

PRINTED IN THE UNITED STATES OF AMERICA

A

BLOCKADED FAMILY

LIFE IN SOUTHERN ALABAMA DURING THE CIVIL WAR

BY

PARTHENIA ANTOINETTE HAGUE

BOSTON AND NEW YORK
HOUGHTON, MIFFLIN AND COMPANY
The Riverside Press, Cambridge
1888

The Riverside Press, Cambridge:
Electrotyped and Printed by H. O. Houghton & Co.

CONTENTS.

———◆———

CHAPTER I.

PAGE

BEGINNINGS OF THE SECESSION MOVEMENT — A
NEGRO WEDDING 1

CHAPTER II.

DEVICES RENDERED NECESSARY BY THE BLOCK-
ADE — HOW THE SOUTH MET A GREAT EMER-
GENCY 16

CHAPTER III.

WAR-TIME SCENES ON AN ALABAMA PLANTATION
— SOUTHERN WOMEN — THEIR INGENUITY AND
COURAGE 31

CHAPTER IV.

HOW CLOTH WAS DYED — HOW SHOES, THREAD,
HATS, AND BONNETS WERE MANUFACTURED . 45

CHAPTER V.

HOMESPUN DRESSES — HOME - MADE BUTTONS
AND PASTEBOARD — UNCLE BEN . . . 61

iv

PAGE

CHAPTER VI.

AUNT PHILLIS AND HER DOMESTIC TRIALS —
KNITTING AROUND THE FIRESIDE — TRAMP,
TRAMP OF THE SPINNERS 76

CHAPTER VII.

WEAVING HEAVY CLOTH — EXPENSIVE PRINTS —
"BLOOD WILL TELL" 89

CHAPTER VIII.

SUBSTITUTES FOR COFFEE — RASPBERRY-LEAF TEA
— HOME-MADE STARCH, PUTTY, AND CEMENT
— SPINNING BEES 101

CHAPTER IX.

OLD-TIME HOOPSKIRTS — HOW THE SLAVES LIVED
— THEIR BARBECUES 113

CHAPTER X.

PAINFUL REALITIES OF CIVIL STRIFE — STRAIT-
ENED CONDITION OF THE SOUTH — TREATMENT
OF PRISONERS 125

CHAPTER XI.

HOMESPUN WEDDINGS — A PATHETIC INCIDENT
— APPROACH OF THE NORTHERN ARMY . . 137

CHAPTER XII.

PILLAGE AND PLUNDER — "PAPA'S FINE STOCK"
— THE SOUTH OVERRUN BY SOLDIERS . 154

CONTENTS.

PAGE

CHAPTER XIII.

RETURN OF THE VANQUISHED — POVERTY OF THE
CONFEDERATES 164

CHAPTER XIV.

REPAIRING DAMAGES — A MOTHER MADE HAPPY
— CONCLUSION 170

A BLOCKADED FAMILY.

I.

On a glorious sunshiny morning in the early summer of 1861 I was on my way to the school-house on the plantation of a gentleman who lived near Eufaula, Alabama, and in whose service I remained during the period of the war.

As I was nearing the little school-room on a rising knoll, all shaded with great oaks and sentineled with tall pines, I heard skipping feet behind me, and one of my scholars exclaiming, "Here is a letter for you, Miss A——! It has just been brought from the office by 'Ed'" — the negro boy who was sent every morning for the mail.

A glance at the handwriting gave me to know it was from my father. I soon came to a pause in the school path: for my father wrote that my brothers were preparing to start for Richmond, Virginia, as

soldiers of our new formed Southern Confederacy. As he wished to have all his children united under his roof, before the boys
went away, my father earnestly desired me
to ask leave of absence for a few days, so
that I might join the home circle also.

The suspending of the school was easily
arranged, and I was soon at home assist-
ing in preparing my brothers for military
service, little dreaming they were about to
enter into a four-years' conflict!

But oh, how clearly even now I read
every milestone of that convulsed period,
as I look back upon it after a quarter of a
century! Our soldiers, in their new gray
uniforms, all aglow with fiery patriotism,
fearing ere they should join battle that the
last booming cannon would have ceased to
reverberate among the mountains, hills, and
valleys of "Old Virginia." The blue cock-
ades streaming in the wind, while Southern
songs, inspirations of the moment, were
heard on all sides : "We conquer or die,"
and "Farewell to Brother Jonathan," leading with fervent ardor.

While the war was in progress, it so
happened that I was far removed from the
seaboard and border States, in southern

Alabama, where our people, encompassed and blockaded by the Federal forces, were most sadly straitened and distressed. It is of the exigencies of that stormy day, as hydra-headed they rose to view, that I have to write; of the many expedients to which we were reduced on our ever-narrowing territory, daily growing not only smaller, but less and less adequate for the sustenance of ourselves, our soldiers, and the Northern prisoners who were cast upon us by the fortunes of war.

Blame us not too severely, you who fought on the Union side; we, too, loved the Union our great and good Washington bequeathed us : with what deep devotion God knoweth. But, as Satan sagely remarks in the Book of Job, "all that a man hath will he give for his life." Also a writer of profane history has truly said that "a man's family is the nearest piece of his country, and the dearest one." Need there be any wonder that, when a political party, with no love in its heart for the Southern white people, came into power, a party which we believed felt that the people of the South were fit only for the pikes hidden at Harper's Ferry, we should have cried out, "What part have we in David? to your tents, O Israel." It is cheering to know that our deeds and intentions have one great Judge, who will say, "Neither do I condemn thee."

I well remember the day when word came with lightning speed over the wires, "The State of Georgia" — my native State, one of the original thirteen of revolutionary fame — " is out of the Union." I also remember that we were by no means elated at the thought that our own noble commonwealth had seceded from the sisterhood of states. Feelings of sadness, rather, somewhat akin to those of the Peri outside the gate of Paradise, overcame us, but we thought and said, Come weal or woe, success or adversity, we will willingly go down or rise with the cause we have embraced. And at that moment an unpleasant recollection rushed to mind, which caused me to think that perhaps, after all, secession was not so very bad. I remembered a temperance lecturer from one of the New England States, who came to our settlement and who was kindly received and warmly welcomed in our Southern homes. There was nothing too good for this temperance lecturer from the far North. He was given earnest and attentive audiences, with never a thought that in the guise of the temperance reformer his one sole purpose was to make a secret survey of our county, to ascertain which settlements were most densely populated with slaves, for the already maturing uprising of the blacks against the whites.

After the failure of the insurrection at Harper's Ferry, we saw with sorrow deepfelt that the three places in our own county which were known to all too well to be most thickly peopled with slaves were marked on John Brown's map of blood and massacre, as the first spots for the negro uprising for the extermination of the Southern whites.

When my brothers had left for Virginia, I started again for southern Alabama, to renew my school duties. As the train sped onward through the tall, long-leaved pines and funereal cypress-trees rising here and there on either side, a feeling of homesick desolation gathered as a thick mist around me, with vague and undefined forebodings of sorrows in store for us.

To add to the depression, clouds dark

and lowering were slowly looming up and spreading themselves over the nether heavens, while low and distant thunder dying plaintively away seemed never before to have fallen so mournfully on my ear. As I looked from the window of the speeding train to the dark green gloom of the almost unbroken forest, the low wail of the wind in the tops of the pines, the lowering dark clouds dimly outlined through the shaded vista, pressed down my heart as with a great sorrow; the far-away mutterings of thunder, the low moan of the wind as it rocked to and fro the tops of the pines, came to me as the Banshee's lonely wail. All seemed to presage some dire affliction. Could it be that my father's household had joined together for the last time in their earthly home? Poe's ghastly, grim, and ancient raven seemed to speak the "Nevermore;" and, alas! nevermore did we children of that happy circle ever meet again.

As the train gathered itself up in the village of Hurtville, the inky black clouds, flashes of almost blinding lightning, and heavy peals of rolling thunder told that the tempest was unchained.

I still had a distance of fourteen or fifteen miles to travel by the hack before I should reach my school. But as the storm began to increase so much in violence, I deemed it advisable to remain in Hurtville for the night. On inquiring for a place to stop at for the night I was directed to Mrs. Hurt, whose spacious mansion and large and beautiful flower yard and grounds stood fair to view from the little village depot.

Hitherto I had passed the village by, in my trips home and back to school again during my vacation days, so that I was altogether a stranger in the home of Mrs. Hurt, but on making her acquaintance was pleased to find her most kind and generous. My quiet satisfaction was further augmented by a loved school companion stepping into the room most unexpectedly, ere I had been seated half an hour. It was a glad surprise for both. Her father and mother lived in the village, and as the violent wind and rain storm had made roads and bridges impassable for the time being, I accepted the invitation of my friend to spend the time of my detention with her.

One pleasing episode of that visit yet

clings to memory. It so happened that
one of the negro girls of the house was to
be married the very week I was detained.
Preparations in various ways had been
making for several days before the celebration of the ceremony. Dear Winnie, if
still a sojourner here, and you chance to
see these lines, I know your memory with
mine will turn back on the wheels of time
to that afternoon, when we were seated on
the colonnade of your father's house. With
flowers scattered all around, our laps and
hands full, we twined the wreath for the
negro girl, the bride elect for the evening.
When twilight had deepened into darkness,
the bride was called into your room to
make ready for the marriage. When fully
robed in her wedding garment, she was
inspected by each and every member of
the household, and judged to be quite *au
fait.* But Winnie pulled off her own watch
and chain, together with her bracelets,
and with these further adorned the bride.
She was married in the wide hall of her
master's house, for having been raised in
the house almost from her cradle, her marriage taking place in one of the cabins was
not to be thought of.

Directly under the supervision of the mistress of the house, a supper that would have been pleasing to the taste of an epicure was served on tables placed out in the smooth gravelly yard. Then after the feasting was over, a round of merry plays, interspersed with the merrier songs and dance, followed. Perhaps no happier beings existed that night. It was like a vision of fairy-land. The full moon chosen for the occasion rode in silent majesty across the star-gemmed heavens ; fleecy white clouds flitted like shadowy phantoms across its silvery path ; the dark pines, half in shadow, half in sheen, loomed vast and giant-like on the outskirts of the village. In the deeper forest could be heard the weird notes of the whip-poor-wills. The pleasing strains of the violin, the thrumming of the banjo, accompanied by many negro voices, awoke the sleeping echoes. From the front colonnade, before us lay the slumbering village all so quietly under the starry firmament. We listened there to the mellow peals of negro laughter, to their strange songs, mingling with the strains of the violin, and the low breathing of the night wind in the forest.

As we roam back in the past, events of
earlier days rise in bright view to mind;
one link in memory's chain runs into another. I cannot forbear here referring to
an incident which occurred a few years
before the civil war. There came to our
settlement from the North, three cultured,
refined, and educated ladies as school-
teachers. Their first Sabbath of worship in
the South was at the Mount Olive Baptist
church, in Harris County, Georgia. The
pastor of the church, for some unknown
cause, failed to appear at the hour appointed for service. We waited for some
time and still no preacher. Then the
good old deacon, known by all as "Uncle
Billy" Moore, who had lived by reason of
strength beyond the allotted threescore
and ten, arose, and said, as the hour for
service was passing, as the minister's arrival seemed doubtful, and as the congre-
gation had all assembled, he would suggest
that Uncle Sol Mitchell, an old and honored negro, preach for us, as he was present, and a member and preacher in good
standing in the Mount Olive church.
There was not even a shadow of an objection to the negro slave's occupying the pul-

pit, as our friends from the far North were witness. Ah, friends of the Green Mountain and Bay State, you will, if yet in the flesh, remember with me that Sabbath so long ago in the South, when the negro slave walked up to the pulpit, opened the hymn-book, and announced the old sacred song:

"When I can read my title clear,
To mansions in the skies."

I remember how loudly my dear father tried to sing — though only a poor singer — just because Uncle Sol was going to preach ; how Sol gave the verses out by couplets to be sung, as was the custom then in the country. All joined in singing that sacred song, and bowed the knee when Uncle Sol said, "Let us pray." I am very sure I have never knelt with more humble devotion and reverence than on that Sabbath morning.

Roads and bridges having been made passable after the storm, I said the "Good-by" to the friends I had found in the pleasant country village, and resumed my journey.

It was a pleasing ride that balmy summer morning, ennobling to the soul, as

nature's great book unrolled its series of
beautiful scenes. Far in the azure blue the
great white banks of clouds seemed to lie
at anchor, so slow of sail were they ; the
gloom of the dense forest, gently waving its
boughs to the morning breeze, would greet
the eye ; the dulcet murmur of gurgling
streams would break on the ear never so
gently ; quiet cottages, surrounded with
flowers and fruits, seemed the abodes of
peace and content. Grass-green marshes
all flecked with flowers of varied tints,
with here and there a tall pine or sombre
cypress standing as sentinels of the bloom-
ing mead ; song-birds caroling their sweet
lays as they flitted from bough to bough,
or lightly soaring in space ; fields of dead-
ened trees, all draped with the long gray
Spanish moss, reminded one of the ancient
Romans mantled with the toga, as they
were silhouetted against the sky ; groups
of great oaks, with clusters of the mistletoe
pendent, calling to mind the ancient Brit-
ons with their strange and terrible religion
of the Druids, when they met together in
their sacred groves for the celebration of
mystical rites.   Now an open field of corn,
green of blade, gently billowed by the wind,

an old gray-haired farmer plowing, seemingly oblivious to all surrounding objects,
and singing, as if from the fullness of a
glad soul, the refrain, " I have some friends
in glory." Ah, honest farmer, thought I,
many of us will join that sad refrain ere
this strife is ended ! On, past a large plantation all in cotton, the clashing of the
many hoes, in the hands of slaves, in uni-
son with the merry songs that floated far
on the gentle zephyrs. The lone country
church gleaming white from a wilderness
of foliage, with its grass green mounds, so
quiet and still. At times the winds came
floating past, laden with the resinous odor
of myriad pines, and filled the surrounding
atmosphere with a sweetness of perfume
surpassing the far-famed incense of Ara-
bia.

In the near distance the home of my
generous employer rose to view, in every
respect the characteristic Southern home,
with its wide halls, long and broad colonnade, large and airy rooms, the yard a park
in itself, fruits and flowers abounding.
Here there was little or nothing to remind
us of the impending conflict. We were
far from the border States and remote from

the seaboard. We had surmised that our
sequestered vale must have been the spot
where the Indian chief and his braves
thrust their tomahawks deep down in the
soil, with their "Alabama, here we rest!"
But soon it came home to us, as the earnestness of the strife began to be realized,
and when we found ourselves encompassed
by the Federal blockade, that we had to
depend altogether upon our own resources;
and no sooner had the stern facts of the
situation forced themselves upon us, than
we joined with zealous determination to
make the best of our position, and to aid
the cause our convictions impressed on us
as right and just. And if up to that time,
in the South, many had engaged in work
purely as a matter of choice, there were
none, even the wealthiest, who had not
been taught that labor was honorable, and
who had very clear ideas of how work must
be done; so when our misfortunes came,
we were by no means found wanting in
any of the qualities that were necessary for
our changed circumstances.

Surely there was work enough to be
done. Our soldiers had to be fed and
clothed; our home ones had to be fed and

clothed. All clothing and provisions for the slaves had to be produced and manufactured at home. Leather had to be of our own tanning; all munitions of war were to be manufactured inside the blockade. The huge bales of kerseys, osnaburgs, and boxes of heavy brogan-shoes, which had been shipped from the North to clothe and shoe the slaves, were things of the past. Up to the beginning of the war we had been dependent on the North for almost everything eaten and worn. Cotton was cultivated in the South almost universally before the war, it was marketed in the North, it was manufactured there, and then returned in various kinds of cloth-material to us.

II.

BUT now the giant emergency must be met, and it was not long ere all were in good training; and having put hands to the plow, there was no murmuring nor looking back. The first great pressing needs were food and clothing. Our government issued orders for all those engaged in agriculture to put only one tenth of their land in cotton, there being then no market for cotton. All agriculturists, large or small, were also required by our government to give for the support of our soldiers one tenth of all the provisions they could raise, — a requirement with which we were only too willing to comply.

In southern Alabama before the war the cultivation of cereals was quite rare. There Cotton was indeed king. I think this saying was true in all the Southern States. It applied to all the territory south of Virginia, Tennessee, and Missouri, at any rate.

When the blockade had inclosed the South, our planters set about in earnest to grow wheat, rye, rice, oats, corn, peas, pumpkins, and ground peas. The chufa, a thing I had never heard of before, now came to the front, and was soon generally cultivated, along with the ground pea, as our position necessitated the production of cheap food for swine. The chufa was easily cultivated, and on fresh sandy or porous soil produced large crops. Every available spot was planted with the chufa, ground peas, and peas. Even in orchards the interstices between the fruit-trees were filled with these nutritious ground nuts. I remember an orchard near where I taught school, planted with chufas. The tubers were dropped about every two feet, in furrows three feet apart. They seemed like great bunches of grass, which spread until the interval between the plants was one mass of green foliage and roots from furrow to furrow. The owners of that orchard said the feed for their poultry had cost them nothing that season, as the whole brood of fowls lived among the chufas from the time they left the perch in the morning till they were called to be housed for the night, and that never before had poultry been so well fitted for the table, never before had the flesh been so white or so well flavored.

Ground peas were rarely grown before the war, and were generally called "goobers." I do not remember that I knew them by any other name; so one day in school hours, when one of the little scholars called to me that "Hetty's got my pindars," I was somewhat mystified as to what a "pindar" was, and when I called the little girl to fetch the pindars to me, she laid two or three goobers in my hand. They were to be seen on all sides, branching out in all directions, in patches large and small. Many planters in giving their corn and cotton the "laying-by" plowing, as it was called, would plant in the middle furrows ground peas, chufas, and cuttings from the sweet potato vines, which required very slight additional labor in harvesting the crops ; and by the time the crops had all been gathered in and frost appeared, the tubers were well matured, and were great helps in fattening pork, thereby enabling the planter to preserve more corn for the use of the government.

Beside growing the ground pea for help in fattening pork, a good supply was housed for seed and the use of the family. I have pleasant recollections of the many winter evenings when we would have the great oven brought into the sitting-room, placed on the hearth, with glowing red coals underneath, filled with white sand, in which we parched the pindars nice and brown. Or perhaps the oven would be filled partly with our home-made syrup, with raw ground peas hulled and dropped into the boiling syrup. Properly cooked, what nice peanut candy that made ! Oil from the peanuts was also expressed for lamps and other uses during war times. In fine, peanuts, ground peas, goobers, and pindars, all one species, though known by all these names, played an important part during the blockade.

Many planters who had never grown wheat before were surprised at the great yield of grain to the acreage sown. I well remember hearing a brother of Mrs. G——, who lived in Troy, Alabama, tell of very highly fertilizing one acre of already rich soil, as a test of what he really could reap from an acre thus treated. The yield went far beyond his most sanguine expectations, for that one acre yielded seventy-five bushels of wheat. Another wealthy planter, living in the village of Glennville, Alabama, had his overseer single out and lay off one acre of very rich hammock land, which was only lightly fertilized, from which he reaped fifty measured bushels. Of course this was only testing what good uplands, or hammocks rich in soil, would yield in wheat by highly or lightly fertilizing. Mr. G—— had sown quite heavily in wheat when all avenues for its entrance to the South had been closed. I remember one twelve acres of hammock land that Mr. G—— had sown in wheat, so rich of soil that no fertilizing was necessary. Morning, noon, and night that twelve-acre hammock in wheat was a topic of conversation at the table during our meal hours. In one of our afternoon rides, when school hours were over for the day, we made haste to view this paragon of a field, and as we halted our horses on the crest of a hill from which we could " view the landscape o'er," what a grand panorama came into view! There, not the " fields arrayed in living green," but wave

on wave of long amber wheat gently rolling in the wind. A large stream of water
bounded two sides of the hammock, and
heavy green foliage formed a background
in vivid contrast to the golden heads whose
every culm seemed on a level. We slid
almost unconsciously from our saddles,
hitched the horses, and were soon standing
in the midst of the wheat, with eyes
scarcely able to peer over that vast plain
of golden-yellow. We took off our hats
and gave them a sail on the already ripen-
ing grain, — for it was near harvest time,
— and there they lay without perceptibly
bending the stalks of wheat. We plucked
some of the grain, rubbed it in our hands
to free and winnow it, and found it sweet
and palatable. Backward flew our thoughts
to that field of wheat near Lake Tiberias
through which Christ and his disciples
passed on the Sabbath day and plucked
the "ears of corn" and did eat, for they
hungered.

The yield of the hammock was estimated
to be at least five hundred bushels; but a
rainy spell set in just as the reaping began,
and it rained in showers, light and heavy,
more or less for twenty-seven days. As

the means then for harvesting wheat were
of a primeval order, the reaping was slow
and tedious, so that most of the grain was
badly damaged, and some was entirely
spoiled.

There was great bother when it came to
threshing the wheat ; many and varied were
the means employed for freeing the chaff
from the grain. Some planters threshed
and fanned the wheat at their gin-houses.
I remember a portable thresher came into
our settlement, and traveled from plantation to plantation, threshing for a percent-
age of the grain. Others, whose sowing
and reaping was on a small scale, resorted
to ruder methods to free the grain, — methods which called to mind the rural life and
manners of ancient times. Sometimes the
wheat was threshed with the rudest sort of
home-made flails.

A woman, whose husband and two sons
were in the army, lived near our settlement
in a cottage which stood some little distance from the roadside, in a cluster of
oaks, whose foliage almost hid the house
from passers-by. While yet some rods
from the dwelling, one day, there came to
our ears a succession of regular thwacks,

the meaning of which we could not define
by the sound. As the woman was a neighbor, we turned aside to investigate, and
opened wide our eyes when we beheld the
woman seated in a chair, with a common
sized barrel just in front of her, within
good striking distance. There she sat, a
sheaf of wheat held with both hands, and
with this she was vigorously belaboring
the barrel, at every stroke a shower of
wheat-grains raining down upon quilts and
coverlets which had been arranged to catch
it. By this simple process she flailed as
much as a bushel or two at one time. She
then spread the sheets out on the ground,
in the open air, and poured the wheat on
them in a continuous stream. The wind
acted as a great "fan," the grain by its
own weight falling in one place, while the
chaff was carried off by the wind. When
that threshing was ground at the flouring
mill and used up, the same rude flailing
was repeated.

Another contrivance for threshing wheat,
even more unique, was that of a woman
whose husband also was in our army. She
was left with five small children, but managed to cultivate a small farm with those of

the five children who had grown enough to
give a little help.   She raised a small plat
of wheat year by year as the war went on.
She had in her smoke-house a large trough
that was used for salting pork when killed
in the winter ; indeed, nearly all smoke-
houses then had large troughs, some as
many as two or three, hewn and dug out
from the stocks of trees, and sometimes
six or eight feet long.   They were very
useful in holding salted pork, salt, soap, and
dried bacon packed down in leached ashes.
The woman cleaned her trough nicely, un-
tied the sheaves of wheat, and placed them
in the trough, not quite brimming, so as to
lose none of the grains ; then with heavy
sticks and little wooden mauls she had
roughly shaped, she and her little children
would beat the grain free of the husks.
It was then winnowed the same way as
was the woman's who threshed over the
barrel.

Hundreds during the war resorted to such
devices for freeing their grain of chaff ; yet
flour was very scarce, although the South
put forth her best energies to cultivate
wheat.   After delivering the government
tithe, and sharing with our home ones,

the crop rarely lasted till another harvest. It was quite amusing to hear the neighbors as they met in social gatherings, or perhaps when separating from service at church, press their friends to come and see them, or come and have dinner, "*For we have got a barrel of flour.*" It was even more amusing to have friends sit at the dining-table, and, when a waiter of brown, warm biscuits was passed round, to see them feign ignorance of what they were.

Bolted meal, when obtainable, made a very good substitute for flour, though millers said it injured their bolting-cloth to sift the corn meal through it ; yet nearly every household, in sending its grist to be ground, would order a portion of the meal to be bolted for use as flour. Such bolted meal, when sifted through a thin muslin cloth and mixed up with scalding water to make it more viscid and adhesive, was as easily moulded into pie crust with the aid of the rolling-pin as the pure flour. Nice muffins and waffles were made of bolted meal, and we also made a very nice cake of the same and our home-made brown sugar.

All the moist and marshy places in the

fields that had hitherto been thought fit for
naught as to the growing of farm products, were utilized for rice and sugar-cane
patches, and were found to yield plentifully.   Some people, not having dank or
moist spots suitable for rice on their
farms, planted rice on the uplands, and
were surprised to find they had an average
yield with those who had planted the moist
spots ; and thus it has come about that
even now in the South rice is planted on
the uplands.   Some few rude rice mills
were hastily put up for stripping the coarse
brown husks from the rice, but as they
were distant from most of the planters in
our settlement, wooden mortars had to be
temporarily improvised.   A tree of proper
size would be cut down ; from the stock a
length suitable would be cut or sawed ; a
cavity would be hollowed with an adze in
the centre of the block endwise.   For the
want of better polishing tools the cavity
would be made smooth by burning with
fire.   The charred surface was then scraped
off and made even, the hollow cleared free
of all coal dust, and the pestle, made, perhaps, from a bough of the same tree, completed the primitive rice mill.   Rough rice

pounded in such a mortar and winnowed by the wind was clean and white. The only objection to it was that it was more splintered than if it had gone through a better mill.

Mills had also to be erected for grinding sugar-cane and the sorghum-cane, as some sorghum was raised in southern Alabama. In our settlement only the "green" and "ribbon" cane were grown, which, like the cereals, were never cultivated before the war. What cane had been grown was in patches owned by slaves, and for the saccharine juice alone. Wooden cylinders had to be used, as those of iron were not easily obtained. With these cylinders all of the juice could not be expressed, but our farmers contented themselves with the thought that there was no great loss after all, as their swine could draw from the crushed cane all the juice that was left before it was hauled to fill ditches and gullies. In case one was so fortunate as to secure a sugar mill with iron cylinders, it used to go the rounds of its immediate vicinity, as the portable threshers did. First one and then another of the neighbors would use it till their crop of cane was

ground and made into syrup and sugar.
The furnaces for sugar and syrup making
were built of rocks, if bricks were not convenient.   They held one or two kettles,
according to the quantity of cane to be
ground and of juice to be boiled.   A
couple or more of long wooden troughs
hollowed from trees were necessary for
containing the syrup when boiled to the
proper degree of density, before turning
into the barrels.   That designed for sugar,
after being turned into the troughs, was
usually beaten with wooden paddles, and
dipper after dipper was filled with the
thick syrup and poured back into the sugar trough, till all was changed into sugar.
Of course there were mishaps now and
then, as evaporators could not be had, and
the planters were not experts in syrup and
sugar making.   I remember one gentleman, whose "green" and "ribbon" cane
had been exceptionally fine for the season,
who had engaged a man who was said to
be something of an expert to supervise his
sugar boiling.   The owner of the cane was
to make his own syrup unaided ; yet his
very first boiling of syrup, when run into

the trough and stirred back and forth with
the wooden paddles to cool, began to crys-
tallize into grains of sugar, and on turning
into the barrel was soon solid, compact,
light-brown sugar, without further stir, and
was his finest sugar, though the one who
supervised, when it came his turn to make
the sugar, tried hard to excel that made
by the merest accident ; but none of his
was so light of color or so free of dripping. Another had boiled his juice too
much for either sugar or syrup, so that he
had a whole barrel full of dark-brown solid
candy, which had to be chipped out with
a hatchet. The syrup that was made
later, as the war went on, was all that
could be desired, — thick, clear, and pure.
The sugar was necessarily brown, as ap-
pliances for refining at that time could
not be had. The planters would place
smooth oak splits and switches in the barrels of sugar, and just the length of the
barrel, to aid the dripping, and to better
free the sugar from moisture. It was not
uncommon to see planters, when they
called upon each other, draw from their
pockets small packages wrapped in our

own manufactured brown paper, which packages contained samples of their make of sugar. These they carried about with them and compared with the sugar made by others.

III.

A WOMAN whose husband and one son were in our army had raised, with the help of her few slaves, among other farm products, a surplus of watermelons. The season had been propitious, and her melons were large, well flavored, and very juicy. So one day she determined to make a trial of the juice of the watermelons for syrup. She gathered those which were thought to be ripe enough for use, prepared a large tub with a sack hanging over it, sliced up the melons, and scraped all the meat and juice into the sack. From what dripped into the tub through the sack when pressed, she managed to get several gallons of bright juice, which she placed for boiling in her large iron kettle — generally known in the country as the "wash pot," and which was always left out of doors, in a shady, convenient place, for washing clothes, making soap, or drying up lard in hog-killing time. She built her fire, boiled the juice slowly, carefully taking off all the scum, and was rewarded with syrup of a flavor as fine, or even finer, than that made from the sugar-cane. Flushed with success, she essayed sugar, also, from watermelon juice, and cakes as nice as those from the sap of the maple were the outcome. The balance of her melon crop was converted into sugar and syrup.

Inasmuch as syrup and sugar had to be placed in barrels, barrel-making was another industry that was forced upon the South. Soon several coopers' shops were built here and there, and it seemed queer enough for us to have home-made barrels, casks, tubs, and piggins. They were manufactured of oak, pine, cypress, and juniper. Those in use for syrup or sugar were generally of oak, as it was thought they gave a more pleasant taste to their contents.

The *Palma christi*, or castor-oil plant, being indigenous to the South and growing most luxuriantly in the wild state, was soon cultivated in patches near our dwellings, for the beans, from which castor oil as thick and transparent as that sold by druggists was extracted. As we had no rollers

to crush the beans, rude mortars were resorted to, in which they were well crushed,
the oil passing, as it was expressed,
through an orifice in the side of the mortar, near its base. Water was then added
to the oil, and the whole was boiled, or
rather raised to the boiling point, which
caused all the impurities to rise to the top,
when it was strained and the oil dipped
from the top of the water. An uncle of
Mrs. G—— had made some castor oil. He
brought her a bottle, and when shown me
I could scarce believe it home-made, as
there was no apparent difference between
this bottle of oil so produced in southern
Alabama and that which we had been
wont to buy before the blockade.

Shoes and leather soon became very
high-priced, bringing home to us the fact
that we had indeed entered on troublous
times. All our planters were reduced to
the necessity of tanning leather for their
own use, and also in order to aid in sup-
plying the soldiers of our Confederacy
with shoes. The home process of tanning
among the lesser planters was perhaps as
crude as that practiced in the earliest
ages ; for although there were many rude

tanneries set in operation during the war, and still ruder modes of grinding the red oak bark for the vats were in vogue in some places, planters on a small scale did not care to carry the few hides they had the long distances to the tanyards. With them the question was how best to tan at their homes, and as the necessity was urgent, it was not long ere they had devised a plan.

The hides were placed in a trough or barrel and covered with water, in which a small quantity of weak lye, that was made to answer the purpose of lime, had been mingled. When the hides had soaked the required length of time, they were taken from the trough, and with but little difficulty and labor the hair was removed and they were ready for the next stage of the process. A pit, of size suitable for the number of hides to be tanned, was dug in the ground near a spring or stream of running water; the bottom and sides were lined with boards riven from the stock of a tree ; the seams were calked tightly with lint cotton, to prevent the tan-ooze from escaping. Then the red oak bark, which had been peeled in long strips from the trees, having arrived, a layer of the bark was placed smooth and even in the bottom of the vat, a layer of hides was stretched over the bark, another layer of bark was put in position, then another of hides, and so on, until the rough vat was filled with hides and bark, — the bark being used just as it came from the trees. Water was poured into the vat, and its contents were left to steep from three to six months, according to the fancy of the tanner. I heard many planters say they had never bought better leather than that which they had tanned by this simple process.

Of course, when neighbor called upon neighbor, the leather that was home-tanned used to be displayed. They would double it over and over again, and often pronounce it the best they ever saw. It made a soft, peculiar noise when pressed with the hands, and was very pliant and supple, answering every purpose for which leather is adapted. Its chief usefulness lay in its furnishing shoes for our soldiers and for those at home, but gear of all kinds used on plantations was mended or made anew from this product ; harnesses for farm use or for equipping army saddles or ambulance trains were manufactured and repaired out of home-tanned leather. And to meet our pressing wants, the hides of horses, mules, hogs, and dogs were all utilized.

One fall, while I was staying at Mr. G——'s, he lost many fine fattening hogs with the cholera. These hogs weighed from two to three or four hundred pounds apiece. It had been his habit to butcher every winter from eighty to a hundred fine porkers. This fall the cholera epidemic had been so fatal that there was scarcely a planter in all the neighborhood but lost a great many swine. They would feed at night and seem to be perfectly well, and be dead by morning; or seemingly well in the morning, and dead by night. As this happened in war time, the loss was felt heavily.

We needed leather so badly that the hogs were flayed as soon as dead, and their hides were tanned. The best and heaviest leather was used for making shoes for the slaves, as their work was out of doors as a rule, and heavy brogans could not be bought. But leather from the hides of swine fell to our lot also, for winter shoes;

and many other white families were obliged
to use it. I remember very plainly when
one of Mr. G——'s daughters and I first
wore swine-skin shoes. They were made of
leather which Mr. G—— himself had had
tanned, and, except that the pores were
very large and wide apart, it looked like
ordinary leather. We had consented with
some reluctance to have these shoes made,
for, although we were willing to immolate
ourselves on the altar of our Southern
Confederacy, it had fallen rather severely
on us to think that we must wear hog-skin
shoes! They were made, however, at a
cost of ten dollars a pair, we furnishing the
leather from which to make them. But
swine-skin leather was very extensible, and
our shoes spread out quite flat by the time
we had worn them a day or so. This was
more than we could endure, so we took
them off, and one of the negro house-girls
came into possession of two more pair of
shoes, while we stepped back into shoes
made of homespun.

As no shoe-blacking or polish could be
bought during the blockade, each family
improvised its own blacking, which was
soot and oil of some variety (either cotton-

seed, ground peas, or oil of compressed lard) mixed together. The shoes would be well painted with the mixture of soot and oil, with brushes made of the bristles of swine. Then a thin paste made of flour, bolted meal, or starch, was applied all over the blackened shoe with another brush, which paste, when dry, gave the shoe as bright and glossy an appearance as if "shined" by the best of bootblacks. Planters were very careful in killing their hogs to save a good supply of bristles, from which shapely brushes were manufactured.

The obtaining of salt became extremely difficult when the war had cut off our supply. This was true especially in regions remote from the sea-coast and border States, such as the interior of Alabama and Georgia. Here again we were obliged to have recourse to whatever expedient ingenuity suggested. All the brine left in troughs and barrels, where pork had been salted down, was carefully dipped up, boiled down, and converted into salt again. In some cases the salty soil under old smoke-houses was dug up and placed in hoppers, which resembled backwoods ash-hoppers, made for leaching ashes in the process of soap-manufacture. Water was then poured upon the soil, the brine which percolated through the hopper was boiled down to the proper point, poured into vessels, and set in the sun, which by evaporation completed the rude process. Though never of immaculate whiteness, the salt which resulted from these methods served well enough for all our purposes, and we accepted it without complaining.

Before the war there were in the South but few cotton mills. These were kept running night and day, as soon as the Confederate army was organized, and we were ourselves prevented by the blockade from purchasing clothing from the factories at the North, or clothing imported from France or England. The cotton which grew in the immediate vicinity of the mills kept them well supplied with raw material. Yet notwithstanding the great push of the cotton mills, they proved totally inadequate, after the war began, to our vast need for clothing of every kind. Every household now became a miniature factory in itself, with its cotton, cards, spinning-wheels, warping-frames, looms, and so on. Wher-

ever one went, the hum of the spinning-
wheel and the clang of the batten of the
loom was borne on the ear.

Great trouble was experienced, in the
beginning, to find dyes with which to color
our stuffs ; but in the course of time, both
at the old mills and at smaller experi-
mental factories which were run entirely
by hand, barks, leaves, roots, and berries
were found containing coloring properties.
I was well acquainted with a gentleman
in southwestern Georgia who owned a
small cotton mill, and who, when he
wanted coloring substances, used to send
his wagons to the woods and freight them
with a shrub known as myrtle, that grew
teeming in low moist places near his mill.
This myrtle yielded a nice gray for woolen
goods.

That the slaves might be well clad, the
owners kept, according to the number of
slaves owned, a number of negro women
carding and spinning, and had looms running all the time. Now and then a planter
would be so fortunate as to secure a bale
or more of white sheeting and osnaburgs
from the cotton mills, in exchange for farm
products, which would be quite a lift, and

give a little breathing-spell from the almost incessant whirr, hum, and clang of the spinning-wheel and loom.

Wide unbleached sheeting was also used for making dresses, and when dyed a deep solid color and tastefully made up the effect was quite handsome. On one occasion, when Mr. G—— had been fortunate in getting a bale of unbleached factory sheeting, Mrs. G—— gave to me, to her two oldest daughters, and a niece of hers, who was as one of the family, enough of the sheeting to make each one of us a dress. We had to hie us to the woods for coloring matter, to dye as each one pleased.

I have often joined with neighbors, when school hours for the day were over, in gathering roots, barks, leaves, twigs, sumach berries, and walnuts, for the hulls, which dyed wool a beautiful dark brown. Such was the variety we had to choose from, to dye our cloth and thread. We used to pull our way through the deep tangled woods, by thickly shaded streams, through broad fields, and return laden with the riches of the Southern forest! Not infrequently clusters of grapes mingled with our freight of dyes. The pine-tree's roots furnished a beautiful dye, approximating very closely to garnet, which color I chose for the sheeting for my dress. A strong decoction of the roots of the pine-tree was used. Copperas of our own production was was used as the mordant. A cask or some small vessel was set convenient to the dwelling-house and partly filled with water, in which a small quantity of salt and vinegar had been mingled ; then pieces of rusty, useless iron, such as plows too much worn to be used again, rusty broken rails, old horse-shoes, and bits of old chains were picked up and cast into the cask. The liquid copperas was always ready, and a very good substance we found it to fix colors in cloth or thread. The sheeting for the dress was folded smoothly and basted slightly so as to keep the folds in place. It was first thoroughly soaked in warm soapsuds, then dipped into the dye, and afterwards into a vessel containing liquid lye from wood-ashes ; then it went again into the dye, then the lye, and so on till the garnet color was the required shade. By varying the strength of the solution any shade desirable could be obtained. My garnet-colored dress of unbleached sheeting was often mistaken for worsted delaine.

Many of the planters in southern Alabama began to grow wool on quite a large
scale, as the war went on and no woolen
goods could be had. All the woolen material that could be manufactured at the cotton mills was used to clothe our soldiers,
so that all the varied kinds of woolen goods
that hitherto had been used with us had
now to be of home hand-make. In this
we achieved entire success. All kinds of
woolen goods — flannels both colored and
white, plaids of bright colors, which we
thought equal to the famed Scotch plaids ;
balmorals, which were then in fashion —
were woven, with grave or gay borders as
suited our fancy. Woolen coverlets and
blankets were also manufactured. The
woolen blankets were at first woven with
the warp of cotton thread, but a woman of
our settlement improved on that by weaving some blankets on the common house
loom, both warp and woof of wool, spun by
her own hands. The borders were bright
red and blue, of texture soft and yielding ;
they were almost equal to those woven at
a regular woolen mill. The process of
weaving all-wool blankets with warp and
woof hand-spun was quite tedious, yet it

was accomplished. Various kinds of twilled woolen cloth were also woven. In weaving coverlets, the weaver had the "draught" before her, to guide her in tramping the pedals and throwing the design of flower, vine, leaf, square, or diamond on the right side. Beautiful carpets also were made on the same plan as coverlets.

Many of the planters, after the shearing of their sheep, used to carry the wool to the nearest cotton mill and have it carded into rolls, to facilitate the making of woolen cloth; and often large quantities of lint cotton were hauled to the factories, to be carded into rolls to be spun at home. But carding rolls by common hand-cards was a rather slow and tiresome process.

IV.

THERE was some pleasant rivalry as to who should be the most successful in producing the brightest and clearest tinge of color on thread or cloth. Most of the women of southern Alabama had small plats of ground for cultivating the indigo bush, for making " indigo blue," or " indigo mud," as it was sometimes called. The indigo weed also grew abundantly in the wild state in our vicinage. Those who did not care to bother with indigo cultivation used to gather, from the woods, the weed in the wild state when in season. Enough of the blue was always made either from the wild or cultivated indigo plant. We used to have our regular "indigo churnings," as they were called. When the weed had matured sufficiently for making the blue mud, which was about the time the plant began to flower, the plants were cut close to the ground, our steeping vats were closely packed with the

weed, and water enough to cover the plant
was poured in. The vat was then left
eight or nine days undisturbed for fermentation, to extract the dye. Then the plant
was rinsed out, so to speak, and the water
in the vat was churned up and down with
a basket for quite a while ; weak lye was
added as a precipitate, which caused the
indigo particles held in solution to fall to
the bottom of the vat ; the water was poured
off, and the "mud" was placed in a sack
and hung up to drip and dry. It was just
as clear and bright a blue as if it had
passed through a more elaborate process.

The woods, as well as being the great
storehouse for all our dye-stuffs, were also
our drug stores. The berries of the dog-
wood-tree were taken for quinine, as they
contained the alkaloid properties of cin-
chona and Peruvian bark. A soothing
and efficacious cordial for dysentery and
similar ailments was made from blackberry
roots ; but ripe persimmons, when made
into a cordial, were thought to be far su-
perior to blackberry roots. An extract of
the barks of the wild cherry, dogwood,
poplar, and wahoo trees was used for chills
and agues. For coughs and all lung dis-

eases a syrup made with the leaves and roots of the mullein plant, globe flower, and wild-cherry tree bark was thought to be infallible. Of course the castor-bean plant was gathered in the wild state in the forest, for making castor oil.

Many also cultivated a few rows of poppies in their garden to make opium, from which our laudanum was created; and this at times was very needful. The manner of extracting opium from poppies was of necessity crude, in our hedged-around situation. It was, indeed, simple in the extreme. The heads or bulbs of the poppies were plucked when ripe, the capsules pierced with a large-sized sewing-needle, and the bulbs placed in some small vessel (a cup or saucer would answer) for the opium gum to exude and to become inspissated by evaporation. The soporific influence of this drug was not excelled by that of the imported article.

Bicarbonate of soda, which had been in use for raising bread before the war, became "a thing of the past" soon after the blockade began; but it was not long ere some one found out that the ashes of corn-cobs possessed the alkaline property essential for raising dough. Whenever "soda" was needed, corn was shelled, care being taken to select all the red cobs, as they were thought to contain more carbonate of soda than white cobs. When the cobs were burned in a clean swept place, the ashes were gathered up and placed in a jar or jug, and so many measures of water were poured in, according to the quantity of ashes. When needed for bread-making, a teaspoonful or tablespoonful of the alkali was used to the measure of flour or meal required.

Another industry to which the need of the times gave rise was the making of pottery, which, although not food or clothing, was indispensable. Of course, our earthenware was rough, coarse, and brown ; and its enameling would have caused a smile of disdain from the ancient Etruscans. Nevertheless, we found our brown-glazed plates, cups and saucers, washbowls and pitchers, and milk crocks exceedingly convenient and useful as temporary expedients, as no tin pans could be had ; and we were thankful that we could make this homely ware.

All in our settlement learned to card,

spin, and weave, and that was the case
with all the women of the South when the
blockade closed us in. Now and then, it
is true, a steamer would run the blockade,
but the few articles in the line of merchan-
dise that reached us served only as a re-
minder of the outside world and of our
once great plenty, now almost forgotten,
and also more forcibly to remind us that
we must depend upon our own ingenuity
to supply the necessities of existence.
Our days of novitiate were short. We
soon became very apt at knitting and
crocheting useful as well as ornamental
woolen notions, such as capes, sacques,
vandykes, shawls, gloves, socks, stockings,
and men's suspenders. The clippings of
lambs' wool were especially used by us
for crocheting or knitting shawls, gloves,
capes, sacques, and hoods. Our needles
for such knitting were made of seasoned
hickory or oakwood a foot long, or even
longer. Lambs' wool clippings, when
carded and spun fine by hand and dyed
bright colors, were almost the peer of the
zephyr wool now sold. To have the hanks
spotted or variegated, they were tightly
braided or plaited, and so dyed ; when the

braids were unfolded a beautiful dappled color would result. Sometimes corn husks were wrapped around the hanks at regular or irregular spaces and made fast with strong thread, so that when placed in the dye the incased parts, as was intended, would imbibe little or no dye, and when knit, crocheted, or woven would present a clouded or dappled appearance. Handsome mittens were knit or crocheted of the same lambs' wool dyed jet black, gray, garnet, or whatever color was preferred ; a bordering of vines, with green leaves and rosebuds of bright colors, was deftly knitted in on the edge and top of the gloves. Various designs of flowers or other patterns were used for gloves, and were so skillfully knitted in that they formed the exact representation of the copy from which they were taken. For the bordering of capes, shawls, gloves, hoods, and sacques the wool yarn was dyed red, blue, black, and green. Of course, intermediate colors were employed in some cases. The juice of poke berries dyed a red as bright as aniline, but this was not very good for wash stuffs. A strong decoction of the bark of the hickory-tree made a clear, bright green on wool, when alum could be had as a mordant ; sometimes there were those who, by some odd chance, happened to have a bit of alum.

There grew in some spots in the woods, though very sparsely, a weed about a foot and a half high, called "the queen's delight," which dyed a jet black on wool. We have frequently gone all of two miles from our home, and, after a wide range of the woods, would perhaps secure only a small armful of this precious weed. We did not wonder at the name, it was so scarce and rare, as well as the only one of all the weeds, roots, bark, leaves, or berries that would dye jet black. The indigo blue of our make would dye blue of any shade required, and the hulls of walnuts a most beautiful brown ; so that we were not lacking for bright and deep colors for borderings.

Here again a pleasant rivalry arose, as to who could form the most unique bordering for capes, shawls, and all such woolen knit or crocheted clothing. There were squares, diamonds, crosses, bars, and designs of flowers formed in knitting and in crocheting.

We were our own wool-sorters, too, and after the shearing had first choice of the fleeces. All the fine, soft, silky locks of wool were selected for use in knitting and crocheting.

Our shoes, particularly those of women and children, were made of cloth, or knit. Some one had learned to knit slippers, and it was not long before most of the women of our settlement had a pair of slippers on the knitting needles. They were knit of our homespun thread, either cotton or wool, which was, for slippers, generally dyed a dark brown, gray, or black. When taken off the needles, the slippers or shoes were lined with cloth of suitable texture. The upper edges were bound with strips of cloth, of color to blend with the hue of the knit work. A rosette was formed of some stray bits of ribbon, or scraps of fine bits of merino or silk, and placed on the uppers of the slippers ; then they were ready for the soles.

We explored the seldom-visited attic and lumber-room, and overhauled the contents of old trunks, boxes, and scrap-bags for pieces of cassimere, merino, broadcloth, or other heavy fine twilled goods, to make

our Sunday shoes, as we could not afford
to wear shoes of such fine stuff every day ;
home-woven jeans and heavy, plain cloth
had to answer for every-day wear. When
one was so fortunate as to get a bolt of
osnaburgs, scraps of that made excellent
shoes when colored. What is now called
the "base-ball shoe" always reminds me of
our war-time colored osnaburgs, but ours
did not have straps of leather like those
which cross the base-ball shoe. Our slippers and shoes which were made of fine
bits of cloth, cost us a good deal of labor
in binding and stitching with colors and
thread to blend with the material used,
before they were sent to the shoemaker to
have them soled.

Sometimes we put on the soles ourselves
by taking wornout shoes, whose soles were
thought sufficiently strong to carry another
pair of uppers, ripping the soles off, placing them in warm water to make them
more pliable and to make it easier to pick
out all the old stitches, and then in the
same perforations stitching our knit slippers or cloth-made shoes. We also had to
cut out soles for shoes from our home-
tanned leather, with the sole of an old shoe

as our pattern, and with an awl perforate the sole for sewing on the upper. I was often surprised at the dexterity with which we could join soles and uppers together, the shoe being reversed during the stitching, and when finished turned right side out again ; and I smile even now when I remember how we used to hold our self-made shoes at arm's length and say, as they were inspected : "What is the blockade to us, so far as shoes are concerned, when we can not only knit the uppers, but cut the soles and stitch them on ? Each woman and girl her own shoemaker ; away with bought shoes ; we want none of them !" But alas, we really knew not how fickle a few months would prove that we were.

Our sewing-thread was of our own make Spools of " Coats' " thread, which was universally used in the South before the war, had long been forgotten. For very fine sewing-thread great care had to be used in drawing the strand of cotton evenly, as well as finely. It was a wearisome task, and great patience had to be exercised, as there was continual snapping of the fine hand - spun thread. From broaches of such spun sewing-thread balls of the cotton were wound from two to three strands double, according as coarse or fine thread was needed. The ball was then placed in a bowl of warm soapsuds and the thread twisted on to a bobbin of corn husks placed on the spindle of the wheel. During the process of twisting the thread a miniature fountain would be set playing from the thread as it twirled upon the spindle. Bunch thread from the cotton mill, number twelve, made very strong sewing-thread, but little could we afford of that; it was exceedingly scarce. When the web of cloth, especially that of factory bunch thread, had been woven as closely up as the sley and harness would permit the warp opening for the shuttle to pass through, the ends of the weaver's threads, or thrums, generally a yard long when taken from around the large cloth beam, would be cut from the cloth and made into sewing-thread. We spent many evenings around the fire, if winter time, or lamp if summer weather, drawing the threads singly from the bunch of thrums and then tying together two or three strands, as the thread was to be coarse or fine. It was

also wound into balls and twisted in the
same manner as other sewing-thread. The
ball would be full of knots, but a good
needleful of thread, perhaps more, could
always be had between the knots.

There were rude frames in most people's yards for making rope out of cotton
thread spun very coarse, and quite a quantity of such rope was made on these rop-
erys. A comical incident occurred at one
of the rope-makings which I attended.
One afternoon, I had gone out in the yard
with several members of the household,
to observe the method of twisting the long
coil of rope by a windlass attached to one
end of the frame, after it had been run off
the broaches on to the frame. Two of the
smaller girls were amusing themselves running back and forth under the rope while
it was being slowly twisted, now and again
giving it a tap with their hands as they
ducked under it, when, just as it was drawn
to its tightest tension, it parted from the
end of the frame opposite the windlass,
and in its curved rebound caught one of
the little girls by the hair of her head.
There was "music in the air" for some
little time, for it was quite a task to free

her hair from the hard twisted coils of
rope.

Our hats and bonnets were of our own
manufacture, for those we had at the beginning of the war had been covered
anew, made over, turned, and changed till
none of the original remained. As we had
no "flowers of sulphur" to bleach our
white straw bonnets and hats, we colored
those we had with walnut hulls, and made
them light or dark brown, as we wished.
Then we ripped up our tarlatan party-
dresses of red, white, blue, or buff, some
all gold and silver bespangled, to trim hats
with. Neighbor would divide with neighbor the tarlatan for trimming purposes,
and some would go quite a distance for
only enough to trim a hat. For the
plumes of our hats or bonnets the feathers
of the old drake answered admirably, and
were often plucked, as many will remember, for that very purpose. Quaker or
Shaker bonnets were also woven by the
women of Alabama out of the bulrushes
that grew very tall in marshy places.
These rushes were placed in the opening
of the threads of warp by hand, and were
woven the same as if the shuttle had

passed them through. Those the width
of the warp were always used. The bonnets were cut in shape and lined with tarlatan.

The skirt of the Shaker was made of
single sleyed cloth, as we called it. In
common woven heavy cloth two threads of
warp were passed through the reeds of the
sley. For the skirts of our bonnets we
wanted the cloth soft and light, hence
only one thread was passed through the
reeds, and that was lightly tapped by the
batten ; it was then soft and yielding.
When the cloth was dyed with willow
bark, which colored a beautiful drab, we
thought our bonnets equal to those we had
bought in days gone by. There was variety enough of material to make hats for
both men and women, palmetto taking the
lead for hats for Sunday wear. The straw
of oats or wheat and corn husks were
braided and made into hats. Hats which
were almost everlasting, we used to think,
were made of pine straw. Hats were made
of cloth also. I remember one in particular of gray jeans, stitched in small diamonds with black silk thread. It was as
perfect a hat as was ever moulded by the

hatter, but the oddness of that hat consisted in its being stitched on the sewing-machine with silk thread. All sewing-machines in our settlement were at a standstill during the period of the war, as our home-made thread was not suited to machines, and all sewing had to be done by hand.

We became quite skilled in making designs of palmetto and straw braiding and plaiting for hats. Fans, baskets, and mats we made of the braided palmetto and straw also. Then there was the "bonnet squash," known also as the "Spanish dish-rag," that was cultivated by some for making bonnets and hats for women and children. Such hats presented a fine appearance, but they were rather heavy. Many would make the frame for their bonnets or hats, then cover it with the small white feathers and down of the goose, color bright red with the juice of poke berries, or blue with indigo mud, some of the larger feathers, and on a small wire form a wreath or plume with bright - colored and white feathers blended together ; or, if no wire was convenient, a fold or two of heavy cloth, or paper doubled, was used to sew the combination of feathers on for wreath, plume, or rosette. Tastefully arranged, this made a hat or bonnet by no means rustic looking.

V.

WILLOW wickerwork came in as a new industry with us. We learned to weave willow twigs into baskets of many shapes and sizes.

A woman of our settlement wove of willow switches a beautiful and ornate body for her baby carriage. As much, she said, to show what she could make out of willow withes, as for the real use of her baby.

The switches were gathered when the willows were flowering, and stripped of bark and leaves ; what was not wanted for immediate use was put by in bundles, to be used in our leisure hours. When placed in warm water the withes were soon as flexible as if freshly gathered and peeled, and were as easily woven into varied kinds of wickerwork.

Mrs. G—— had a flock of sixty or seventy head of geese. A large stream of clear water ran within a stone's throw of the rear of the dwelling, through what was the

main pasture-lot for the geese. Clear pools
of water, caused by the sudden bend of the
stream, rocks, or perhaps a fallen tree, were
formed as the stream wound through the
pasture-lot, in which the geese were nearly
all the time swimming. This kept their
feathers snowy white. Wishing a finer
grade of fans than we had made of braided
palmetto or woven rushes or pasteboard,
it was not long ere we had learned to put
the secondary wing-feathers of geese to
that use. When the feathers were " ripe "
we would pluck them, being very careful in
the plucking to string on a strong thread
the feathers one by one as they were taken
out. All the right wing-feathers were
placed on one string, the left wing-feathers
on another separate string, so that when
we were ready to arrange the feathers for
making fans, each feather would be in its
proper place, just as drawn from the wing
of the goose, and would therefore have the
fitting curve. The secondary feathers of
both wings were used to make one fan.
Its handles were of cedar or pine wood
and were sometimes made on the "turn-
er's machine," but oftener we whittled
them out of cedar or pine wood ourselves.

They were always covered with scraps of velvet, silk, cassimere, or merino, and bits of old faded ribbon dyed some bright color. We soon became adepts in the art of making fans out of the wing-feathers of geese, and beside those for our own use we made and sold many in the city of Eufaula for ten, fifteen, and twenty dollars apiece.

A sister of Mrs. G——, who lived some little distance from us, and who owned a large flock of pea-fowls, often favored her sister with the more valuable dark olive-green wing-feathers of her magnificent birds, and they made superb fans. I was remembered by Mrs. G——, and was given a select pair of wing-feathers. I gave my best skill to this fan, for it was to be a present to my mother. The handle I covered with a piece of dark green silk velvet for which I exchanged a scrap of silk of a different color, so as to have an exact blending of the feathers and silk velvet for covering the handle. On either side where I had joined the handle and feathers, I placed a rosette made of the small green and blue variegated feathers that adorn the neck and breast of the pea-fowl. Two buttons cut out of pasteboard and cov-

ered with a bit of the silk velvet, saved
from covering the handle, were placed in
the centre of the rosettes. I think it would
have been difficult to have singled out that
fan as not imported. I was offered thirty
dollars for it as soon as it was completed.
One would scarcely believe how beautiful
our snow-white fans of geese feathers were,
with their large rosettes on either side,
made of the blue and green small feathers
that grace the neck of the peacock. We
made fans also of gray goose feathers, and
from feathers out of turkeys' wings and
tails were made strong substantial fans, for
every-day use in summer.

An amusing incident happened one day
while we were making fans of the feathers
of the geese. We had been told by some
one that if we would tie a strip of scarlet
cloth around a goose's neck, it would fly
away and never return. Late one afternoon the oldest daughter of the house and
I were strolling all alone in the pasture-lot
where the geese were feeding on the luxuriant grass. At sight of the sleek, glossy
flock feeding *en masse*, the impulse arose
on the instant to put to the test the roman-
tic hearsay, and we quickly caught a goose

of snowy whiteness. My companion then took off her crimson silk belt (a relic of ante-bellum days). We tied it around the anser's neck, kneeling on the soft carpet of grass, one holding the goose by the wings, while the other adjusted the belt ; then we loosed it, expecting to see the spread of wings that was to bear it from our sight forever. But nothing of the kind happened. It stepped cautiously around with its neck gracefully curved as if endeavoring to divine the mystery of the crimson streamer, while the entire flock without a single exception set up a hissing and cackling that was almost deafening, and with necks extended began to chase the goose with the scarlet pennant. The loud cackling of the flock awoke the quiet of the house, and soon a negro girl came running, sent by her mistress, to see what was disturbing the geese. The legend had proved false ; but we wondered not, as we retraced our steps, that the loud cackling of a flock of geese in Rome betrayed the presence of the Gauls who were about to storm the citadel.

Mrs. G—— promised her two older daughters, her niece, and myself a new

home-woven, home-spun dress, just so soon
as we should jointly finish the make-up of
the slaves' fall and winter clothing, which
we joined hands forthwith in cutting out.
Two suits apiece of heavy goods were
made for their winter wear, and two suits
apiece of material not so heavy for their
spring and summer wear. It usually took
from six to eight weeks of cutting out and
sewing to get all the slaves into their new
garments. We were ever willing to lend
our aid in the make-up of the negroes'
clothing, yet the promise of a new homespun dress, to be dyed and woven as best
pleased us four, aroused our latent energy,
and we soon completed the task without
once knowing fatigue. Then our homespun dresses came to the front. There
was much consulting, advising, and draught-
ing by the four, before we had decided as
to the color, check, or stripe we should
have our dresses dyed or woven. I well
remember the color, stripe, and check —
together with the spangles that were woven
in the meshes of thread — that we each
made choice of. The warp was the same
for all four dresses, — nearly solid drab,
with the exception of a narrow stripe of

white and blue threads in a group, for every twelve or fourteen threads of drab, running parallel to each other the whole length of the warp. The drab was dyed with the bark of 'the willow-tree. The hanks of thread for the woof of my dress were closely plaited and dyed a deep, clear blue with our home-made indigo. When woven it presented the appearance of " cirro-cumulus " clouds. The niece and one of the daughters betook them to the garret to rummage amongst antique silk and woolen garments much " the worse for wear." Part of an old black silk, and some red scraps of merino, and a remnant of an old blue scarf, was what they decided upon as spangles for their dresses, and both were to be just alike. The black silk and red and blue were cut into narrow strips ; the strips were again cut into bits from a quarter to half an inch in length and woven in the meshes of thread the whole length of their dresses.

The black, blue, and red bits of color were placed in by hand, varying from an inch to two or three inches apart. Sometimes the bits of bright color were placed in so as to form a square, diamond, or cross ;

sometimes no order or method was heeded,
but they were placed in on the "crazy"
plan ; yet when all the tiny bits had been
placed in and when the material was made
up into the dress, it presented quite a
spangled appearance. The other daughter
had hers woven of solid drab, of willow-bark
dye, and with a narrow stripe of blue and
white running the length of it in the warp;
and this was just as pretty as the rest of
our dresses, that had given a deal of
trouble.

Buttons for our dresses were our next
consideration, and we had quite a debate
on this weighty subject, as our substitutes
for buttons and material for making them
were many and varied. It was something
bewildering for us to determine finally what
sort of buttons we should adopt.

Rude machines were devised for making
buttons of wood as the war went on, and
we were thrown more and more upon our
own resources. The buttons made of wood
were of various sizes, and were strong
and lasting for heavy goods, especially
the clothing for the slaves. Sometimes
we would get the wood buttons, polish
them with a bit of sandpaper, and varnish

them with a little of the copal varnish
that happened to be on hand when the war
began, and which was being carefully hus-
banded; our buttons thus polished and
varnished exhibited some likeness to those
we had been wont to buy in palmier days.
Many a household manufactured its own
buttons. They were made of cloth cut
round, and of as many ply as was necessary for firmness. Thick, heavy button-
hole stitches were worked all around the
edge with thread coarser than the cloth of
which the button was made, and when
these were stitched on firmly there was no
worry about the washerwoman's breaking
or washing them off.

Thread that we spun at home was used
for making buttons. The process was simple. A small reed, or, if that was wanting,
a large-sized broom-straw, could be used;
around this the thread for such buttons
would be wound till of sufficient bulk; it
was then slid from the reed; the button-
hole stitch was used here again, and was
thickly worked around the eyelet made by
the reed; the eyelet was crossed with
thread stronger than that of which the button was formed, for the purpose of attach-

ing it to the garment. Persimmon seeds
were also used for buttons with very good
success, for being of such a tenacious and
solid substance they could be put on clothing that required washing. Very nice buttons were also shaped out of pine bark,
and were covered or not, just as one liked,
but these were useless on garments for
wash. The shell of the common gourd
was almost universally used at the South
for buttons during the period of the war;
when covered with strong homespun cloth
they could stand washing. Pasteboard was
also used to make buttons. We have often
cut in different shapes and sizes pasteboard and the shell of the gourd for buttons. We would have them round, oval,
square, or diamond shaped, then cover
neatly with cloth, with scraps of silk, or
with fine pieces of colored woolen goods,
to match whatever material was used for
dress or basque.

Our pasteboard was made in our own
homes. I smile even now when I think of
that crude process. We used old papers
and worn garments and a paste made of
flour, or bolted meal sifted through fine
cloth. A paper was spread on a table,

paste was spread evenly and smoothly over the surface of the paper, a layer of cloth just the width and length of the paper was laid on, another coating of the paste followed, and so on, alternating with paper, paste, and cloth, until the required thickness was reached; then with a hot smoothing-iron the whole was pressed till perfectly dry, smooth, and glossy, and we had pasteboard adapted for all household needs.

But to return to our buttons. They were made of drab thread, and after we had thickly worked the button-hole stitch around the eyelet, each took thread colored to blend with the warp and woof and again lightly overcast the button, so that the drab showed only as the background. The older daughter and I overcast ours with blue thread; the other two overcast theirs with red thread. It was then fashionable to place straps on the shoulder seams of ladies' dresses, with generally from four to six buttons on the straps. We placed straps on ours, trimmed with the buttons which we had made, and they added not a little to the finish.

We had intended to wear our new homespuns to the village church the Sunday

after completing them. Perhaps there was
the least bit of vanity in our thoughts of
how we should appear in church in our
first home-woven suits ; palmetto hats that
we had braided and made with our own
hands ; slippers that we had knit, with
soles cut out of our home-tanned leather,
and on which we had with our own hands
joined uppers and soles together.   But

> " The best laid schemes o' mice and men
> Gang aft a-gley."

It was Saturday night, and our new dresses
had been pressed with the smoothing-iron
all so nicely and hung on hooks alongside
the wall, so as to avoid any unnecessary
creasing.   All four of us hung up the
dresses with especial care just before we
stepped into the dining-room to have our
suppers. "Eliza and Mary always have
something new and unusual in the make of
their homespun dresses," thought we, " but
they shall be surpassed to-morrow.   Both
teacher and pupils were at an age then
when the heart is keenly desirous for
beauty and effect.

Uncle Ben was the negro man who
drove the carriage, made fires night and
morning in all the rooms of the house,

hoed the garden, helped Aunt Phillis, the
cook, who was his wife, and did chores in
general around the house and yard. Now
it happened, as Aunt Phillis afterward told
us, that Ben had made his plans for that
very Sunday also. He was to meet by
agreement with the negroes of contiguous
plantations in a swamp not far distant
from the negro quarter on Mr. G——'s
plantation, to engage in games with
cards. Their masters of course knew
naught of it, for they would not have permitted it. In passing round the house
and yard Uncle Ben heard us say we were
going to the village church that particular
Sunday, and that we should be sure to
wear our new home - woven suits. He
knew he would have to drive the carriage,
and I suppose he thought if it had not
been for our new dresses of the home-
made cloth, like as not we would not want
to drive ; for often we did not use the carriage on Sundays, but preferred walking
to the quiet country church and Sabbath-
school scarce a mile from my employer's
residence.

While we were all at the supper-table
that Saturday night, Ben, as usual, was

making the round of the rooms, replenish-
ing all the fires.   He reached our room.
There were the four dresses hanging plain
to view, and he thought of having to drive
the carriage on the morrow.   One of the
little girls had taken a bath and left a
large basin of water, with the sponge in it,
near the fire-place.   Ben gathered up the
sponge, pressed some of the water from it,
wiped the soot from the chimney's back,
and smeared our prided homespun garments to his heart's content!   Then he
carefully disposed the skirts so as to ef-
fectually conceal the smut.   It being Saturday night, he expected that we could not
have the much-soiled dresses ready for
Sunday's wear, even if we should discover
the smut that evening.

When we went back to our rooms from
the supper-table our first glance was toward our much-valued dresses, which appeared to hang just as we had left them.
But before we had seated ourselves, surprise was manifested at some large flakes
of soot on the hearth and floor and near to
our precious garments.   One of us called
attention to the sponge, which was almost
black, floating in the basin of water.   The
fire, beginning to burn anew, showed the

chimney's back almost free of soot, and
scarcely dry from the sponge. Thinking
no harm had befallen our homespuns, I
casually touched the folds of mine, when
several flakes of soot fell to the floor. Immediately I loosed wide the folds of the
skirt, when, lo! such a smut never before
nor since have I seen, from waist line to
the hem, one whole width all begrimed
with soot. The other girls flew in a trice
to their dresses, and as quickly unloosed
the folds of their skirts. Lo! behold, it
was smut, smut, soot, soot, broad and
long! We knew in an instant it was Ben,
for he was often "contrary" about driving
the carriage, especially if he had made
plans for his own amusement. Irritation
and disappointment were the prominent
feelings at first, augmented by the thought
that our homespuns would never look de-
cently again, but our vexed feelings soon
gave way to ringing laughter as we pic-
tured to ourselves Uncle Ben in the midst
of smutting our dearly-prized garments.
He deserved punishment, surely, but beyond a good scolding no correction was ad-
ministered, although Aunt Phillis declared
that "Massa orter half kill Ben fur sicher
mean trick."

VI.

ONE blustering, drizzling March night
at our home in Alabama the two little
daughters of Uncle Ben and Aunt Phillis,
who, since their early childhood had been
brought up in Mr. G——'s house as ser-
vants, came rushing into our room with
the startling intelligence that "Daddy's
arter mammy; he's got an axe in his hand
and says he's gwine ter kill her dis berry
night." Where Phillis was hiding the little girls knew not. She was not in the
kitchen, nor in her cabin; neither had she
come into the house to her master and
mistress. "Her's dodgin' 'round to keep
out'en daddy's way," the younger of Phillis's girls declared. We all became deeply
interested in Aunt Phillis's troubles, and
dropped our knitting and crocheting in
severe disapprobation of the way in which
Ben was treating his helpmate, and our
censure was the more emphasized when
we remembered the smutting he had given

our dresses. The smaller boys and girls of the household came also into our room to hear Martha and Maria tell of Ben's chasing Phillis around with the axe, and soon we had ten all told around the fire, all gathered close together.

The mournful echoing and reëchoing of the March wind as it rushed past in fitful, heavy gusts, sometimes rattling the window panes, then dying away through the dark pine forests that bounded one side of the mansion, added not a little to our excited imaginings, and we lapsed into a kind of dread silence, when all of a sudden an unearthly scream came from just beneath our feet, it seemed, and we sprang up instantly. Martha, who had recognized her mother's voice, at one bound passed through our room door to the rear hall door, which she opened in a twinkling and Aunt Phillis flew into our room. We slammed the door to on the instant, thinking Uncle Ben was at his wife's heels, and that one of us might catch the hurl of the axe intended for Phillis. We braced our shoulders against the door with all our strength, but Uncle Ben was prudent enough not to try to force an entrance.

Mrs. G——, hearing our screams, imagined that the house had caught fire. She sped to our room and reached the door just as we were in the act of slamming it shut, so that it caught her left hand just across the knuckles, and she was held all of a minute before she could make herself heard in the great uproar. The third finger of her left hand was badly crushed, and to this day shows the imprint of that accident. Mr. G—— also hastened to our room, and, finding that Ben was after Phillis with an axe, got his gun, and from the rear hall door peered forth into the bleak night for Ben ; but no Ben could be seen or heard. When the Babel-like confusion of our tongues had somewhat stilled, Aunt Phillis was called upon to explain her piercing scream. She said that as she was putting her kitchen in order for breakfast in the morning, Ben had told her he was going to split her head open that very night with the axe, and went to the wood-pile for the axe. Then Aunt Phillis slipped round on the front colonnade next her mistress' room, thinking if Ben should come for her there she could quickly spring into that room. From the

front colonnade she saw Ben go into the
kitchen axe in hand. Not finding her
there, he came out again and went to the
rear of the house. Although the night
was dark, she imagined her dress was of
light enough color to betray her to Ben,
should he come on that side of the house.
She then thought of our room, which, on
account of an incline in the yard toward
the front gate, was not raised as high off
the ground by two or three feet as the
rooms on the front colonnade. Aunt Phillis reasoned that if she crept under the
house as far as our room, where a good fire
was always burning in the winter time,
she could keep warm seated at the base of
the chimney, and if need be, sleep there all
night, secure from the fury of Ben. So
she crawled as far down as our room, and
made herself as comfortable as the ground
would permit, chuckling the while at Ben's
prowling around for her in the raw March
wind and rain. She was the more content
as she knew her two girls slept in her mistress's room. To use her own words, " I
was gitten good and warm 'gin the bricks
o' de chimbley, and feeling sort o' sleepy,
soon was nodden. I jest happened to

open my eyes as I raised my head of a sudden, and bless God! dar was Ben crawlin' right up to me on his knees, wid de axe in his hand. I tell yer, I never knows how I did got out fro' under dar."

Uncle Ben, despite his eccentricities, lives yet on the old plantation with his mistress; but Mr. G—— died years gone by now. No one bears any ill-will, I am sure, to venerable Uncle Ben, not even those of us who well remember his misdeeds; and this episode of those days of civil strife — an episode connected with the two oldest daughters of Mrs. G——, her niece, and myself, — stands out with clear distinctness, though more than twenty years have gone.

While knitting around the fireside one night, talking of what we had done, and could yet accomplish, in industries called into existence by the war and blockade, we agreed then and there that each of us four could and would card and spin enough warp and woof to weave a dress apiece. This proved a herculean task for us, for at that time we barely knew how to card and spin. Mrs. G—— smiled incredulously, we thought, but kindly promised to have the dresses dyed and woven, in case we should card and spin them. The older daughter and I elected to work together. I was to card and spin eighteen yards of warp — nine yards of our wide heavy homespun being then ample enough for one plain dress. Of course we used the same style the whole four years of the war, in our secluded settlement ; not a fashion plate or "ladies' magazine" did we see during that entire period, so that we were but little troubled as to "latest styles." My companion in work was to card and spin eighteen yards of filling. Similarly the other daughter and her cousin agreed as to carding and spinning their warp and woof. We imposed the number of cuts each should spin, agreeing that each should spin one cut every night after our suppers, Saturday night excepted. Every Saturday we were to card and were spin six cuts apiece, till eighteen yards finished.

Inasmuch as it took about six cuts of our soft spun woof to make one yard of thick heavy cloth, and about the same of hard twisted warp, we were not long in numbering the weeks we should be in spinning the four dresses ; and of course, going to school or teaching school, and spinning only nights and Saturdays, our progress on the eighteen yards was necessarily slow. We thought, however, that we would have them ready for the loom in ten weeks at the farthest. Mrs. G—— said if we had them ready to dye and weave in three or four months we would do well. But there were those who could card and spin from one to two yards of cloth per day and do it easily.

On a certain Monday evening, after we had supper, we began quite merrily the carding and spinning for our four dresses, and made our first cut of thread by the number of rolls we had carded and spun. I remember that seventy rolls carded evenly and smoothly, if of medium size, would reel one cut of thread. We invariably added two or three rolls to the seventy for good measure. Our rolls at first were oddly shaped, often evoking ridicule, but we soon learned to mould them to perfection.

Our first Saturday to spin was looked forward to with great expectations by the four, as six cuts were marked down for

that day. I smile even now, as memory
wanders back over the tide of years, to
think how, all during the week preceding
that Saturday, I was resolving in my mind
to far outstrip the number of cuts imposed
as our task. I kept this resolution all to
myself, inwardly chuckling at the grand
surprise I was to give them all when the
day's work should be finished ; and I did
give a surprise, too, but in a way that was
by no means pleasing to me.

The eagerly wished for Saturday dawned.
Two spinning-wheels and two pair of cotton-cards, with a basket of nice white lint
cotton, were set in our room before we had
risen from bed, according to orders de-
livered the evening previous ; and as the
sun rose the hum of the spinning-wheels
began, as we had the night before carded
enough rolls to supply us with material.
Two would be carding rolls and two spinning, and by alternating between carding
rolls and spinning, we rested, both as to
standing and sitting, discoursing meanwhile what color, or what variety of colors,
these self-spun dresses should be dyed ;
whether plain, plaid, checkered, or striped
they should be woven. Now and then the

monotony would be enlivened by snatches of song ; merry laughs and jests went round ; first one and then another of us would cry out above the never - ceasing humming of the wheels, " I know I shall have my six cuts by the time the sun is down ;" and I thought to myself, but did not give voice to the words, " Should n't wonder if I have seven cuts or more, when the sun sets."

Steadily all that Saturday was heard the tramp, tramp, as we marched up and down the floor beside our spinning-wheels. We were glad indeed to see the sun sinking like a huge ball of fire behind the green-topped pines, plain to view from the windows of our room. That evening the words, " The night cometh, when no man can work," had for us a new meaning. We were more joyful, I believe, as the eve was drawing on, than we had been at dawn. We were wearied, but were in a fever of anxiety to know the result of our steady labor. So diligently had we applied ourselves that two carded and spun while two were at dinner ; there had been no cessation of our work.

When the sun set, the whirring ceased,

and gathering up our broaches which looked like so many small pyramids, we marched Indian file to the sitting-room for Mrs. G—— to reel the thread we had spun. Our broaches had to be placed in a basket for the thread to be run off as it listed. There was "a scientific way" of running the thread on to the bobbins, which were of corn-husks or thick paper, and placed on the spindle of the wheel for the thread to be run on to form the broach. Any one at all experienced in spinning could so run the thread on the broach that in reeling, the broach being held at the base by the hand, the thread would run smoothly off the apex of the broach without ever a break or tangle to the very last strand. We had not run our thread on the broaches with the same amount of skill we had shown in spinning, hence there was much difficulty in reeling, but before we had finished the thirty-six yards of cloth our broaches ceased to give annoyance.

It was decided by all in the room that my broaches must be the first reeled, — how strangely these names sound now, then familiar household words, " broach," "reel," " hank," " rolls," " card," " warp," " web

of cloth," and so on ! With no little pride
I saw my great day's work sailing round
on the reel. At every one hundred and
twenty rounds, a sharp click of the reel,
and one cut would be told. A thread was
looped around that cut, to separate it from
the next cut. But as the reel gave the
second sharp click, and that cut was looped,
I saw with dismay that what was left of my
broaches would barely reel another cut. I
almost held my breath as the third cut was
flying round. "Shades of Pallas !" thought
I, "am I to have only three cuts ?" Alas !
click ! only three cuts and a few strands of
thread over. How glad I was that I had
not voiced in the household my being so
sure of seven or more cuts ! All were
quite mystified for a few moments to know
why after such a day's carding and spinning I should have fallen so short of the
task allotted each one, and which was
fairly within our power. Some of the girls
were saying "I think I won't have my
broaches reeled." Mrs. G——, meanwhile,
was giving my small hank the necessary
loops around the reel before removing, and
when she did remove my hank from the
reel it rolled a ball of kinks in her hands.

Having been warned that the warp, to make it strong, required much more twisting than filling, but being an entire novice in the art, I had given the thread I spun entirely too much twist, — had really put six cuts in three, so that, after all, I had not done so bad a day's work, and could join as heartily as the others in ridiculing my ball of kinks, as it passed from one to another for inspection.

The other warp spinner had not given her thread enough twist to answer for warp, so that it had to be used for woof. Mrs. G——, dear motherly woman that she ever was, knowing how assiduously we had applied ourselves to the card and wheels, and wishing to give encouragement to our undertaking, gave to each of us unfortunates eight cuts of warp so that we also closed that Saturday night rejoicing with the other two spinners, who had made just their number of cuts. But as I lay down to sleep, it was with the thought that the twelve labors of Hercules were as nothing compared to the eighteen yards of warp-thread which I had given my pledge to card and spin.

As the novelty of carding and spinning

wore off, we often grew weary in our strife, and it is not to be denied that all four of us became heartily sick of our agreement by the time we had carded and spun two weeks at night and two Saturdays, and never another Saturday dawned that found us so eager to spin as did the first one. Each of the four felt inclined to withdraw from the compact, but that was never acknowledged until victory had crowned our efforts.

VII.

As no muslin could be bought for summer wear, and our home-made cloth was very heavy and warm for hot weather, we women of southern Alabama devised a plan for making muslin out of our own homespun thread; and the fact that it was made of this thread added not a little to its excellence in our estimation.

In the weaving of all heavy, thick cloth, whether plain or twilled, two threads, sometimes three, were always passed through the reeds of the sley, when the warp was put in the loom for weaving the web of cloth. The experiment for muslin, and it proved quite a success, was to draw the threads of warp singly through the reeds of the sley. In the process of making muslin, both warp and woof were sized with sizing made of flour, to make the threads more smooth and unbending; whereas plain cloth had only the warp sized, and that with sizing made of Indian-meal.

When thread for the muslin was beamed,
and one single thread passed through the
reeds of the sley, and only a slight tap of
the batten given as the shuttle passed
through the opening with its quill of sized
thread, the texture was thin and gauze-like,
and stood out like any real muslin stiffened
with starch.

The thread for our muslins was dyed a
deep plum color.   In the case of each of
our four dresses, the warp was the same:
twelve or fourteen threads of the plum color
and three threads of white alternating with
the plum color and white thread the width
and length of the cloth.   The older daughter and I had ours filled in solid with plum
color, which, with the narrow white stripes
in the warp, made a very neat dress.   The
two other girls had theirs checked with
white, so as to form a square with the
white stripe in the warp ; then small bits
of crimson merino were placed in the centre of the square.   Our muslins reminded
me of "Swiss muslins," with their raised
flowers of silk or fine wool thread.   When
we first appeared in them, they were mistaken for the genuine imported muslins.

Soon after completing and wearing our

home-made muslins, news came into our
settlement that a steamer had run the
blockade, and that the city of Eufaula had
secured some bolts of prints and other notions.   The Saturday following the report,
Mr. G—— ordered Ben to harness up the
horses, and we were driven to Eufaula, not
to buy, but simply to have a look at these
imports.   Sure enough, on the shelves in
the store that had long lain empty, there
were tastefully disposed a few bolts of Eng-
lish prints, some ladies' straw hats, a bolt or
two of fine bleached stuff, some calico, and
a few pairs of ladies' shoes.   These were
the magnets which had drawn us eleven
miles !   We had fondly imagined ourselves
satisfied with our home-made cloth, and
had said of it, as David of the sword of
Goliath, " There is none like that ; give it
me."   When we had held aloft our knit and
cloth-made shoes and slippers, with the
words, " What do we care for the blockade
when we can make such as these ? " we
had little dreamed that our firmness would
so suddenly collapse before about three
bolts of calico and a few pairs of black morocco shoes, lined with red and deep blue
leather, laced high and scalloped around

the top edge. Yet so it was, for when the
merchant unfolded to our view his brand-
new prints, looking so fresh and novel, we
four had nine yards apiece cut off, paying
twelve dollars per yard for it. It was
something over a yard wide, and as we
knew nothing of the ruffling, puffing, plaiting, tucking, or shirring of overskirts or
polonaises outside the blockade, nine yards
were amply sufficient for a dress.

The design of that print is yet vivid to
my memory. The background was a pale
blending of violet with white ; the fore-
ground was dotted with violets of a deep
purple color. I bought the same day a
plain brown straw hat, paying one hundred
dollars for it, and a half quire of small
white note-paper for forty dollars. A pair
of morocco gaiters cost one of the daughters three hundred and seventy-five dollars.
We surely will be pardoned, if we felt some
pride in wearing muslins that we had manufactured with our own hands, and fresh new
calicoes which had cost each of us one hundred and eight dollars.

Our neighbors, as soon as it was noised
about in that quiet settlement (where it
seemed almost impossible for tidings of

the outside world to come) that we had
new store-bought calicoes, all paid us a visit
in order that they might see how a new
print looked amidst so much home-woven
cloth ; and a bit of the scraps left was given
each visitor. I sent a small scrap of my
new calico — our war-time calicoes, as we
then and afterward called them — in a letter to my relatives in Georgia. Whenever
any one was so fortunate as to secure a
new print, small scraps of it were sent in
letters to friends and relatives, so rare were
new calicoes.

Indeed, it was not at all uncommon for
friends or relatives to send small samples
of new homespun cloth to one another in
letters whenever what was thought to be a
particularly good pattern had been devised,
or the colors were exceptionally brilliant.

A woman who was a neighbor of ours
made herself what really was an elegant
dress for the times. The material was an
old and well-worn black silk dress, altogether past renovating, and fine white lint
cotton. The silk was all ripped up, and
cut into narrow strips, which were all rav-
eled and then mixed with the lint cotton and passed through the cotton cards

two or three times, so as to have the mixture homogeneous. It was then carded
and spun very fine, great pains being
taken in the spinning to have no unevenness in the threads. Our neighbor managed to get for the warp of her mixed silk
and cotton dress a bunch of number twelve
thread, from cotton mills in Columbus,
Georgia, fifty miles from our settlement,
and generally a three days' trip. She
dyed the thread, which was very fine and
smooth, with the barks of the sweet-gum
and maple trees, which made a beautiful
gray. Woven into cloth, it was soft and
silky to the touch, and of a beautiful color.
It was corded with the best pieces of the
worn silk, and trimmed with pasteboard
buttons covered with some of the same
silk.

Some very rich-appearing and service-
able winter woolen dresses were made of
the wool of white and brown sheep mixed,
carded, spun and woven just so ; then long
chains of coarser spun wool thread dyed
black and red were crocheted and braided
in neat designs on the skirt, sleeves, and
waist of these brown and white mixed
dresses of wool.

Of course braid and tape could not be bought, nor could we weave that sufficiently narrow to make a neat appearance on dress goods ; but we soon found that long chains of crochet-thread would answer nicely for braiding. Balls of it were crocheted of various colors ; black, white, red, blue, and dark brown were the colors most used. It was braided on in various ways ; sometimes singly, at times we would sew three or four chains together of colors to blend, making the tape an inch or more wide. And thus it was placed upon our dresses.

The extent and variety of our cloth manufacture, our fertility in making designs, our different ways of weaving, were really remarkable. We made cloth in stripes broad and narrow, and in checks wide and small. We made plain cloth, twilled cloth, jeans, and salt-and-pepper cloth, the latter by alternating one thread of white and one thread of black the width and length of the warp, and the same in the woof. This was a slow process, as the shuttles, with the quills of black and white thread, were changed at every tap of the batten. Plaids were woven both of wool and cotton thread. They required three

and four shuttles and as many varieties of
color. We had "dice"-woven homespun,
or "basket plait," as some would call it,
which required three or four treadles and
as many different ways of tramping them
to form the plait. When the warp was
dyed a solid red or deep garnet and filled
in with blue, or perhaps purple, slate, or
black, as one wished, or when the warp
was dyed blue and filled in with whatever
other color pleased the eye, such cloth we
called our "chambrey."

Sometimes lint cotton was dyed a deep
and a pale blue, and then carded and spun
as dyed. If the warp was of deep blue the
woof would be pale blue ; or the woof
would be deep blue thread and the warp
pale blue. It was woven solid and tipped
with bright bits of silk, cassimere, merino,
or other fine woolen scraps, which, cut in
small pieces, were woven in the meshes of
thread.

Cloth was woven with two, three, four,
and five treadles. An ingenious way the
weaver had of tramping the treadles would
throw up on the right or upper side of the
cloth whatever design was placed in front
of the weaver's eye. Some beautiful car-

pets of wool, dyed a variety of bright colors, were woven on our common house-loom ; and large woolen coverlets as well as woolen and cotton flannels were made in the same manner.

I often wonder how we were able so quickly to adapt ourselves to the great changes rendered necessary in our modes of life by the blockade. But be it remembered that the Southerners who were so reduced and so compelled to rely entirely upon their own resources belonged to the Anglo-Saxon race, a race which, despite all prating about "race equality," has civilized America. The reflection to which memory gives rise when I recall war times in the South is this, that "blood will tell."

As to our cotton flannel, while it was rather heavy for every-day wear, it was just the thing for capes and cloaks, and was often made into blankets. The filling was spun rather coarse and very softly twisted. If it was to be used for capes or cloaks the raw cotton was dyed whatever color was made choice of before carding and spinning ; if the flannel was to be used for blankets the lint cotton was carded and

spun white. When placed in the loom
for weaving the treadles were tramped in
a manner which threw up the coarse, soft
spun woof very nearly all on the upper
side of the cloth. Two or three heavy
beats of the batten were given to pack the
filling close and dense. When so much
had been woven and was still smoothly and
tightly drawn over the breast-beam, one
of a pair of cotton-cards was used by the
hand to raise the lint of the coarse, soft-
twisted, tightly-packed filling, till it was
perfectly smooth and downy. It would
then be passed over the cloth-beam, and
again so much would be woven ; then it
left the loom-bench, and with the card the
lint was raised again in the same manner.
And so the process of weaving and stop-
ping to raise the lint with the cards would
go on to the end of the warp. It was a
slow and tedious way of making cotton
flannel, but a large quantity was made.
That which was dyed a very dark brown,
and with which great pains had been taken
in raising the lint, was, at some little distance, sometimes mistaken for sealskin.
So much for the ingenuity of the women
of southern Alabama.

Soon after we had finished our self-imposed task of carding and spinning the warp and woof for our four dresses, and it had been noised far and wide in our neighborhood that we had had patience to hold out until the task was completed, one of our acquaintances, a young lady, set to to excel us, in that she was not only going to card and spin the warp and woof for a new homespun, but was herself going to weave the thread she had spun into cloth for her dress. She finally arrived at the loom with her warp and woof and commenced with great joy the weaving. Her homespun warp proved to be quite defective. There were more or less broken threads to mend in the run of any warp, even that spun at the cotton mills, which was always stronger than hand-spun warp. At first, when the threads of warp would break on either the cloth-beam or thread-beam side, she would leave the loom-bench and mend the broken threads ; but she became impatient and wearied at the oft-breaking threads (sometimes three or four would snap asunder at once), and by the time she had woven three or four yards she had tired altogether of mending and piecing,

so she began to leave the threads hanging
wherever they happened to snap apart,
and soon a thick fringe of thread was
hanging from the sides and middle of the
cloth on both sides the harness and sley.
She kept on weaving, however, saying she
had enough for the plain skirt, and, as it
narrowed, that would cut the waist, and
if it narrowed yet more, why that would
make the sleeves; but the more threads
that broke the fewer were there to sustain
the remaining ones, so that the cloth, from
being a good yard wide at the beginning,
narrowed to less than half a foot, and after
the first two or three yards was useless for
any purpose, and there ended that homespun that was to be the wonder of the
settlement.   We felt nowise inclined to
exult over our friend's failure, for we no
doubt would have suffered defeat had we
attempted .to weave our spun warp.   It
required no little patience to work with
warp the threads of which were every now
and then breaking, for every thread had to
be mended as soon as it broke, or if not,
thin, flimsy places would occur all through
the web, and the cloth would not wear long
enough to pay for the trouble of carding,
spinning, and weaving.

VIII.

ONE of our most difficult tasks was to
find a good substitute for coffee. This palatable drink, if not a real necessary of life,
is almost indispensable to the enjoyment
of a good meal, and some Southerners took
it three times a day. Coffee soon rose to
thirty dollars per pound ; from that it went
to sixty and seventy dollars per pound.
Good workmen received thirty dollars per
day ; so it took two days' hard labor to buy
one pound of coffee, and scarcely any could
be had even at that fabulous price. Some
imagined themselves much better in health
for the absence of coffee, and wondered
why they had ever used it at all, and declared it good for nothing any way ; but
"Sour grapes" would be the reply for such
as they. Others saved a few handfuls of
coffee, and used it on very important oc-
casions, and then only as an extract, so to
speak, for flavoring substitutes for coffee.

There were those who planted long rows

of the okra plant on the borders of their cotton or corn fields, and cultivated this with the corn and cotton. The seeds of this, when mature, and nicely browned, came nearer in flavor to the real coffee than any other substitute I now remember. Yam potatoes used to be peeled, sliced thin, cut into small squares, dried, and then parched brown ; they were thought to be next best to okra for coffee. Browned wheat, meal, and burnt corn made passable beverages ; even meal-bran was browned and used for coffee if other substitutes were not obtainable.

We had several substitutes for tea which were equally as palatable, and, I fancy more wholesome, than much that is now sold for tea. Prominent among these substitutes were raspberry leaves. Many during the blockade planted and cultivated the raspberry-vine all around their garden palings, as much for tea as the berries for jams or pies ; these leaves were considered the best substitute for tea. The leaves of the blackberry bush, huckleberry leaves, and the leaves of the holly-tree when dried in the shade, also made a palatable tea.

Persimmons dried served for dates.

Each household made its own starch, some of the bran of wheat flour. Green corn and sweet potatoes were grated in order to make starch. This process was very simple. The grated substance was placed to soak in a large tub of water; when it had passed through the process of fermentation and had risen to the surface, the grated matter was all skimmed off, the water holding the starch in solution was passed through a sieve, and then through a thin cloth to free altogether from any foreign substance. A change of clear water twice a day for three or four days was made to more thoroughly bleach the starch. It would then be put on white cloth, placed on scaffolds in the yard, and left to drip and dry. Starch of wheat bran was made in the same manner. It was as white and fine as any ever bought.

A good makeshift had soon been devised for putty and cement, and the artlessness of it will perhaps cause a smile to flit across the face of glaziers. But no cement could be bought, and this was useful in many ways, as panes of glass had to be set in, or a break to be mended; the handle broken from a pitcher to be placed on

anew, or repairing done to table ware.
When it was necessary to repair any such
breaks, a Spanish potato (none other of
the species of that esculent root answered
so well) was roasted in hot ashes, peeled
while yet hot, immediately mashed very
fine, and mixed with about a tablespoonful of flour; it was then, while warm, applied to whatever need there was. This
paste, when it had become hardened, remained fixed and firm, and was as durable
as putty.

In place of kerosene for lights, the oil
of cotton seed and ground peas, together
with the oil of compressed lard, was used,
and served well the need of the times. For
lights we had also to fall back on moulding
candles, which had long years lain obso-
lete. When beeswax was plentiful it was
mixed with tallow for moulding candles.
Long rows of candles so moulded would be
hung on the lower limbs of wide-spreading
oaks, where, sheltered by the dense foliage
from the direct rays of the sun, they would
remain suspended day and night until
they were bleached as white as the sperm
candles we had been wont to buy, and almost as transparent as wax candles. When

there was no oil for the lamps or tallow for moulding candles, which at times befell our households, mother-wit would suggest some expedient by which the intricate problem of light could be solved.

One evening at a neighbor's, where we had gone to tea, when we took our seats at the supper-table we were diverted by the lights we were to eat by, the like of which, up to that time, we had not seen, nor even thought of.

In the absence of any of the ordinary materials for lighting, the good woman of the house had gone to the woods and gathered a basketful of round globes of the sweet-gum tree. She had taken two shallow bowls and put some lard, melted, into them, then placed two or three of the sweet-gum balls in each of the vessels, which, soon becoming thoroughly saturated with the melted lard, gave a fairylike light, floating round in the shallow vessels of oil like stars.

At other times rude lamps or candles were improvised, anything but attractive in appearance, though the light was fairly bright. Medium-sized bottles (of course any proper sized bottle would answer) were taken, and several strands of spun thread twisted together to form a wick two or three yards long were well steeped in beeswax and tallow, and coiled around the bottle from base to neck closely and evenly. When ready for lighting, one or more of the coils of thread would be loosed from the bottle, raised above the mouth an inch or so, and pressed with the thumb to the neck of the bottle. When the wick had burned to the bottle's mouth, the same process of uncoiling and pressing the wick to the bottle would be repeated. This gave a steady flame. When beeswax could not be had, tallow was used for steeping the strands.

Sewing societies were formed in every hamlet, as well as in our cities, to keep the soldiers of the Confederacy clothed as best we could. They met once every week, at some lady's house, if it was in the country. To such societies all the cloth that could be spared from each household was given and made into soldiers' garments. Socks, gloves, blankets, woolen coverlets, and even home-made bedquilts were donated ; wool scarfs, knitted on long oak or hickory - wood needles, were sent for our soldiers in the bitter cold of Virginia, to wrap around their necks and cover their ears.

In many settlements there were spinning "bees." Many women whose husbands were in the army found it uphill work to card and spin all that was necessary to clothe a numerous family, In such cases, as often as was needful, there would be a gathering of ladies of the settlement, both married and single, for the "spinning bee." Wheels, cards, and cotton were all hauled in a wagon to the place appointed. On the way, as often as not, a long flexible twig would be cut from the woods, and attached to one of the spinning-wheels ; from the top of such flagstaff would play loosely to the wind, and jolts of the wagon, a large bunch of lint cotton, as our ensign. Sometimes as many as six or eight wheels would be whirring at the same time in one house, and assistance was also given in weaving, cutting out, and making up clothing for such families.

Ah, those stormy days of our convulsed country had their guileless pleasures, as well as sorrows ! We were drawn together in a closer union, a tenderer feeling

of humanity linking us all together, both
rich and poor; from the princely planter,
who could scarce get off his wide domains
in a day's ride, and who could count his
slaves by the thousand, down to the humble tenants of the log-cabin on rented or
leased land.   I have now a letter written
by a Southern woman, whose husband and
oldest son belonged to an Alabama regiment, which was ordered to Island No. 10,
in the Mississippi River; and soon surrounded there as it was by the Federal
army, communication was cut off between
our soldiers and the home ones.   Soon the
island was captured by our enemies, and
her husband and son were taken prisoners.
She was then thrown upon her own resources entirely to provide for a family of
ten, no longer receiving the government
pay of eleven dollars per month each for
husband and son.   Her two oldest daughters were large enough to give her some
help in her battle to keep the wolf from the
door.   These people were of those who
had never owned a slave in their lives, and
who had but a few acres of land, but they
were just as true and devoted to our cause
as those who numbered their slaves and

acres by the thousand. I cannot forbear quoting here a few lines of this brave, good woman's letter.

" We had a hard time [she writes] ; myself and two oldest daughters making a living for ten in the family. There was no work the little boys could do. We spun and wove cloth to sell, day by day, and we took in sewing, which was done by night. We knit a great deal, and worked, oh, so hard! and I thank God that it was so, for had it been otherwise, had I had time to sit and ponder over all the sad details that the daily news brought me, I should have failed. But when night came on, my weary, aching limbs and troubled heart were soon at rest ; and I awoke refreshed, and ready for another day's trials; and I am proud to say we never went to bed hungry. . . . We even had some merry days, neighbors and friends meeting together, telling our trials, and even laughing at them ; feeling that the sacrifice was little, could we but gain our cause. There is one thing I am proud of, and that is, the advantages we took of our resources, and our own independence. I can hardly see how such a people could be conquered."

She lives to-day in the "Lone Star" State, surrounded by nine of her children, who are all good and useful citizens. Her husband died in a Northern prison. The oldest son, who was taken prisoner when his father was, was paroled soon after the South's surrender, and returned home, as thousands of others did, to join a broken home circle.

We often thought, and said too, that it was well for us all in the South that our minds were so taxed in devising temporary expedients, and our hands so busied in carrying them into effect; we really had no time to brood over the sorrowful news that the papers were daily depicting. We were being led in a way we knew not : and like the humble woman of the cottage, we even made merry over our inevitable privations and inconveniences. Indeed, we grew so accustomed to them that they scarcely seemed privations.

While hemmed in on all sides by the blockade, we used to think that if no war were raging, and a wall as thick and high as the great Chinese Wall were to entirely surround our Confederacy, we should not suffer intolerable inconvenience, but live as happily as Adam and Eve in the Garden of Eden before they tasted the forbidden fruit. We used to say, " How can we be subdued, when we have so cheerfully and uncomplainingly given up every luxury, and in a measure even the comforts of life ; and yet with what crude resources are at hand, we are feeding and clothing the whole people of the South, civil as well as military ?" We felt all the more pride, when we remembered that at the beginning of hostilities we were unprepared in almost every essential necessary to the existence of our Confederacy ; yet now, the best part of two years had gone, and the South was holding her own.

Our day of adversity had not come; it was not unnatural that we sang with fervor and animation, "We conquer or die," and " Farewell, Brother Jonathan." But we did not forget to call upon the Lord in the day of our success, as well as in the day of our adversity. Often the inhabitants of our settlement — and it was just the same all over the Southern States — were called to the house of worship to sanctify a fast. What comfort and consolation we gathered from the reading of the first and second

chapters of the book of the Prophet Joel;
how fervently and devoutly we prayed that
God would stay up the hands of our armies,
till victory was won; and trusting God we
would return lifted up in spirit to our homes
and to our labor. It was well for us that
we had not prophetic vision to foresee the
result of the contest. We fasted, we prayed,
we trusted; but victory did not crown our
armies.

IX.

It may excite some amusement to record the fact that among the thousand and one industries and makeshifts which blossomed into life in southern Alabama during the period of the war, the making of hoopskirts, which were worn extensively before, as well as during, and even for some time after, hostilities between the North and South, was not neglected. One of the ladies of our county devised a means of weaving the hoopskirt on the common house-loom. It mattered not if the tapes were all broken, and the casing all worn off the steels, a new farthingale was warranted, if only the steels of the worn skirt came.

There were raids made upon garrets for all old broken-up hoopskirts and pieces of steel belonging to such skirts, which we either carried or sent to the renovator of dilapidated hoopskirts. Her first move was to tightly wrap the steels one by one

with homespun thread, three or four
strands double, but not twisted, piecing
the steels, when necessary. An old hoopskirt not so worn was her guide as to the
proper number and length of steels. The
thread for the warp of the skirt was passed
through the harness eyes and reeds of
the sley about an inch wide, which was to
answer for the tape of the skirt ; a space
of threads, six or more inches, was skipped
in the harness and sley ; the thread for the
tape again passed through the harness and
sley ; another skip, and so on the length of
the sley. When ready for weaving, one of
the encased steels was placed in the openings of the narrow strips of warp, the steel
projecting about three inches on each side
of the outside tape ; the steel was woven in ;
then about two inches or more of tape was
woven ; another steel was placed in ; the
same length of tape woven ; another steel,
and so on till all the steels required for the
skirt were woven in. The space of tape for
the top of the skirt was then woven, and
half of the skirt was finished. The other
half was woven in the same manner ; the
projecting ends of the steels were joined
and closely wrapped, and the hoopskirt was

complete so far as the weaving was concerned.

These skirts were neat and satisfactory
when finished off by hand. The weaving
was slow and difficult, however, because
the shuttle could not make a clean shoot
through the narrow openings of warp, but
had to be passed through each one by
hand. The maker above referred to was
another humble cottager whose husband
and son were in our army, and to use her
quaint expression, she was trying "to make
both buckle and tongue meet," while husband and son were fighting for our cause.

It was really ridiculous, our way of making raids upon what remained of our fine
bed-linen, pillow-shams, and slips, for garments of finer texture than our own home-
woven cloth. I well remember that once,
when I stepped into a friend's room, her
very first words were, "This is the last
bleached, seamless bed-sheet I've got, and
now I must cut it up for garments!" I
doubt very much if a fine sheet could have
been found in any house in our settlement
when the war closed. Perhaps there was
not one in the blockaded South.

Fine white pillow-shams were cut up and

made into white waists, to wear with our
heavy home-made skirts in the hot summer.
Sometimes a family would happen to have
a bundle of scraps of blue striped bed-tick-
ing, which would be divided around among
the neighboring girls. We would ravel it
all up, taking care to save every blue
thread (which was a fast color) to em-
broider flowers on the front, collar, and
cuffs of our white waists, made of pillow-
shams and slips ; and we did think them
beautiful and prized them all the more
highly because of the narrow pass to which
we had arrived for fine material to tide us
over till our cause should be won ; and if
we used up all the fine sheets, pillow-slips,
and shams of ante-bellum days for our
wear, soft home-spun, home-woven sheets
took their place.

Cloth that was called thirded was woven
for sheets and pillow-slips. Two threads
of warp would be passed through the reeds
of the sley for all plain or twilled cloth.
For single sleyed cloth one thread only
was passed through the sley-reeds. For
cloth woven "thirded" the weaver would
begin by drawing two threads through the
first reeds of the sley and one thread

through the next reeds, two threads again, and then one, thus alternating the width of the warp two and one. When filled in with soft fine-spun filling, this stuff was soft and yielding, and easy to handle in the wash.

Some real nice towels were woven of the thirded cloth, and edged with wide or narrow blue borders of our home-made indigo, as that was ever a fast color. A fringe would be formed at both ends of the towel by raveling out an inch or so of the woof; they had to be inspected closely to note the difference between them and those bought in the usual manner.

Many of our women, when cotton was at its prime in opening, and before any rain had fallen on it, would select and pick themselves from the bolls that were the longest and fullest of the white fleecy staple, enough for their finest knitting purposes. They would also pick the seed from the white silky locks with their fingers, which would spin a longer, finer thread than if it had been ginned. I have seen socks and stockings knit of such prepared cotton that, in point of fineness of texture, were almost the equal, and in lasting power were more than the equal, of those bought at

stores.   One of my pupils, who is yet living in southern Alabama, prepared enough
of such thread with her own hands to give
me as a present, with the expressed desire
that I should knit for myself a pair of stockings.   I used very fine knitting needles, and
took great care to draw every stitch on
the needles so as to have no unevenness.
Three or four inches above the instep I
commenced knitting " shell-work," which
was in fashion then.   We could not have
our hose as fine as that which we had once
bought, but we tried to cover that defect
by all manner of fancy designs in knitting,
such as " leaf and vine," " clock-work,"
" shell-work," and plain or twisted " ribs."
These covered all the upper part of the
foot, and had they been knit of fine white
floss they could not have made a better appearance.

Another article which we learned how
to produce was " hair oil."   We had plenty
of roses, fragrant ones too, which we gathered, and then filled quite a large bowl
with their petals, among which we put
enough fresh, white hog's lard to fill the
bowl to the brim.   When melted, a piece
of glass was placed over the bowl securely ;

it was then put on a scaffold out in the yard,
where the rays of the sun could shine down
upon it all day. There it remained for two
or three weeks day and night, until the
petals became crisp and transparent. The
mixture was then strained through a thin
muslin cloth into a mug or other small
vessel, and we were content with it, knowing that it contained nothing deleterious
to the scalp or hair.

Although war was raging all around,
both on sea and land, yet in our quiet valley which, we were vain enough to believe,
rivaled the far-famed Vale of Cashmere,
everything moved on the even tenor of its
way. We were happy and contented, both
master and slave. Late on Saturday af-
ternoons, the weekly rations for the slaves
were given out ; and in addition to them
would be given for Sunday cheer, flour,
lard, butter, sugar, and some substitute for
coffee, as real coffee had been given before
the war. They had the privilege also of
vegetables and fruits. On Sundays the
slaves would do their own cooking. On
week days a negro slave was regularly
detailed to cook for the laboring hands,
and even provender for the plow stock was

placed in the feed troughs by the "trash-gang," as they were called, composed of negro boys and girls not old enough for regular field work. On week days the laborer had only to take the gear off the mule and turn it in the lot gate, and then go to dinner ready waiting for him.

Farmers not owning more than fifteen or twenty negro slaves generally had all the cooking for white and black done at the same time. I have often heard farmers say since the war, and laugh over it, that they had really eaten no good cabbage, turnips, or collard - greens since slavery times. It used to be necessary to cook so much bacon for the slaves that vegetables and "greens" of any variety were well seasoned. During the war when bacon was very scarce, it often happened that the white household would deny themselves meat to eat, so as to give it to the slaves, as they had to toil in the field.

If a negro was sick, a doctor, who was already paid, was called in all haste, as planters used to engage a doctor by the year, at so much for each slave whether large or small.

One negro boy called " Jim," about eighteen years of age, was quite sick of a fever one fall. His master and mistress had him brought from the "quarter" over to the dwelling - yard and placed in the cook's cabin, so that he might be given close attention. One or the other watched him day and night (for he was a very valuable boy) and gave the medicine. One Saturday during his illness his master had to go to the city for some purpose, and he asked me to help his wife and daughter care for Jim that day, saying, as he stepped into his buggy, "Now be careful of Jim, and see to it that he lacks for nothing; if he dies, I 've lost one thousand dollars, good as gold." It was nothing uncommon then for able - bodied young negro men to be valued at from one thousand to eighteen hundred dollars. If Jim be living to-day, I know he has not forgotten our giving him his medicine and gruel at the regular hours, heating hot bricks and placing them at his feet as the doctor ordered, nor how I burned my fingers muffling the hot bricks.

Very often the sick negroes would be brought right into their masters' houses, so as to be more closely watched.

Then there were the annual barbecues that each and all planters gave without fail to their slaves when the crops had all been laid by, which semi-holiday weeks embraced the last of July and the first of August. I remember in particular one barbecue roast that I witnessed one night in company with the household. The "pits" were some little distance from the mansion, and were half filled with red-hot coals of oak and hickory wood, over which the flesh of whole dressed beef, mutton, and shoats were slowly roasting, lying on a grate made of split staves of oak or hickory wood. A goodly-sized vessel, containing vinegar, butter, salt, pulverized sage, pepper, and thyme, all mingled together with a "swab," stood in close proximity to the barbecuing meat. Every now and then the roasting flesh would be turned over with long oak sticks sharpened smoothly to a point at one end, which answered the place of forks ; deep and long incisions would be made in the barbecuing meat, and with the swab a good basting of the mixed condiments from the bowl would be spread over ; the process of turning the roasting flesh over the glowing red coals

and basting with the seasoning continued
till the meat was thought to be thoroughly
done. It would sometimes be far beyond
the hour of midnight before the barbecuing meat was removed from the "pits,"
and I yet think that such barbecued meats
cannot be surpassed by any other sort of
cooked or roasted meats. When cold and
sliced, it was certainly delicious. A night
barbecuing was a weird scene. Blazing
pine-torches heaped on the rude stands
improvised for the occasion threw a ruddy
glow out over the dark forest, giving an
uncanny aspect to the long thick moss
swaying sylphlike in the night breeze.
Some of the negroes would be tending the
roasting flesh ; some with the swab, basting with the seasoning ; some laughing
loud enough to wake the sleeping echoes ;
some lazily stretched out on the ground
thinking of to-morrow's feast. Now and
then some one would "pat Juba," as they
called it, while the dim light of the moon
and stars peeping through the heavy foliage, together with the savory smoke rising
from the pits, enhanced the strangeness of
the fête.

When the morrow came, two or three

long tables were set in the far-reaching
shade of grand old oaks, whose every
limb was hung plentifully with the long
gray moss that is so common in the southern part of the Southern States, and which
imparts to the trees in that section an aspect strikingly patriarchal.

The tables would be weighted with the
flesh of the ox, mutton, pork, and great pans
of chicken pies, as well as fruits, vegetables,
and light bread and cakes of our bolted
meal. Seats were arranged all around, and
old and honored negroes, called to preside
at the heads of the tables, would bid them
all to seat themselves, — by fifties, it often
was, — when, with hands uplifted, they in-
voked the divine blessing.

Many in southern Alabama yet retain a
vivid recollection of these regular annual
barbecues, given to the slaves when the
crops had all been " laid by."

X.

OFTEN have we sat on the colonnade of
that lovely Alabama home, and wondered
if any part of the world could be more
beautiful. We would number the stars at
night as they peeped forth one by one, in
the clear blue vault above, until they became innumerable, and then the full moon
would deluge the whole scene with its shin-
ing flood of light. Or perhaps it would be
in the deepening twilight, when the heavens were unrelieved by moon or star, that
the soul would be touched, as the drowsy
hum of nature's little wildwood insects
came stealing gently on the ear. Not infrequently the mocking - birds would trill
their varied notes, or we would hear the
faint tinkle of bells as " the lowing " herds
wound "slowly o'er the lea." In the distance the negro plowmen were returning
homeward chanting their " corn song."
Ah ! but those old " corn songs " had mel-
ody then ! They lent enchantment to all

the surroundings. Even yet they call from
out the misty shadows of the past a host
of memories, when they fall upon ears
that were wont to listen to their quaint refrain in days gone by.

Often Uncle Ben, on the colonnade or
in the hall, would while off on the violin
that his master had given him pleasing
plantation melodies, accompanying his per-
formance with his rude singing. He would
seem almost transported with ecstacy, as
he used to stand with head thrown back,
eyes shut, and foot vigorously keeping
time ; and often as he drew forth his art-
less strains a dozen or more negroes, old
and young, would be dancing in the white,
sandy yard, as merrily as " birds without
barn or storehouse."

Sometimes, in the solemn hush of the
closing Sabbath eve in the country, sweet
strains of song would float out upon the
air from the negroes' quarter. Many large
planters had preachers employed to teach
and preach regularly to the slaves. One
Sabbath night I yet remember above all the
others. Our day of gloom was drawing on,
we could no longer close our eyes to the
fact that our cause was drooping ; our sol-

diers were meeting with reverses on all sides, hope was only faintly glimmering. Cast down and disquieted as we were that night, the services at the negro church made a deep impression upon our minds. They sang an old time song, the refrain of which we could just catch. When they began the first verse, —

> " Where, oh where is the good old Daniel?
> Where, oh where is the good old Daniel?
> Who was cast in the lion's den;
> Safe now in the promised land."

When they would strike the refrain, —

> " By and by we 'll go home to meet him,
> By and by we 'll go home to meet him,
> Way over in the promised land,"

we could almost imagine they were on wing for " the promised land," as they seemed to throw all the passion of their souls into the refrain, and fancy would almost hear the rustle of wings, as the deep swelling anthem rolled forth. Again it would be, —

> " Where, oh where is the good Elijah?
> Where, oh where is the good Elijah?
> Who went up in a chariot of fire;
> Safe now in the promised land."

And the chorus, —

> " By and by we 'll go home to meet him,"

would peal forth again in loud - shouting
strains. I hushed my breath to hear the
mellow strains of that song, and seemed to
see the mantle of our lost cause descend-
ing.

It was about this time that a letter came
from my father, saying one of the soldier
brothers was at home on a twenty-one days'
furlough. This was the first home-coming
since the commencement of hostilities in
1861. My presence was again desired at
home, to meet with the long - absent
brother. But by some irregularity of the
mail, it so happened that my letter had
been delayed, and I saw by the postscript
and date that my brother would be leaving
for the front again before I could possi-
bly reach my father's house. Yet a great
yearning came over me, on reading his
kindly letter, to see my father again. Soon
I was homeward bound once more, disap-
pointed and pained at not being in time to
see my brother. I gave little heed to the
landscape spread out as the train swept
onward ; but my heart gave a glad bound
when the waters of the Chattahoochee
river, sparkling in the bright sunlight,
greeted my eyes, for now I should soon be
at my father's house.

Here and in all the surrounding neighborhood, as far as I could see, the same vigorous efforts were put forth to feed and clothe the soldiers of our Confederacy, as well as the home ones, that I had witnessed in southern Alabama. There was the same self-sacrifice, without a thought of murmuring for the luxuries enjoyed before the war. Yet with the nicest economy, and the most studied husbandry, — however generously the earth might yield of grain, fruits, and vegetables, — the South was awakening to the painful reality that the produce grown on our narrowing space of Confederate soil was inadequate for the sustenance of those at home, our soldiers, and the Northern soldiers whom we held as prisoners. We were not only encompassed by land and water, but the Confederacy was divided in twain by the gunboats of the Federals on the Mississippi River. With nearly all the soldiers from west of the Mississippi River in the eastern half of our Confederacy, we had no communication whatevever from beyond the great " Father of Waters." All aid and succor as regarded provisions and clothes for our army was at an end from beyond the Mississippi. We were caged up like a besieged city. There was neither egress nor ingress for men or means. Our soldiers from the west had to share what little provisions were grown in our circumscribed limit. They also shared what clothing could be manufactured in the more and more straitened condition of the South.

If a soldier from the west drew a furlough he could not get to his home. Those who had relatives or friends east of the Mississippi River would spend their leave of absence with them. Sometimes the soldier from the west would give the furlough he drew to some friend he had made on this side ; or perhaps it would be that the soldier of our side of the river would send his comrade of the west to his people and home with a letter of introduction.

I remember a good man and neighbor, who lived near my school, who had four grown sons in the army, one by one killed outright in battle, one at Fort Donelson, one at the battle of Franklin, in Tennessee, another near Chattanooga, the last and youngest at Chickamauga. A while before the last two were slain, one had drawn a furlough to come home, but there being in his regiment a comrade from the State of Texas, to whom he was very much attached, and who was by no means well, though on duty, this son had the furlough he had drawn transferred to his Texas comrade, whom he sent to his father's with a letter of introduction, asking for his Texas friend the same welcome that would have greeted himself.

Mr. Saunders, the Texan, came, and was welcomed in Mr. Weaver's family as warmly as one of his own sons would have been, the more kindly by the family and all the neighborhood because he was debarred from visiting his own home. He spent three weeks in our settlement, and returned to camp much invigorated in health and spirits. In less than six months, both the sons were slain in battle, and a few weeks afterwards Mr. Saunders also fell and was buried in north Georgia.

My employer also had Texas relatives in our army, who came on their leave of absence to his home. They could not so much as hear from their own homes.

To make our situation worse, all the rice-growing lands of Georgia and South Carolina were overrun by Northern troops;

and all the negro laborers of the large rice
plantations, as well as those lying contiguous to the rice-growing districts, had
been decoyed off by Federal troops, which
more and more crippled the eastern half
of our Confederacy, which was then bur-
dened with the whole Confederate army,
as well as thousands of Northern prisoners,
to say nothing of the Federal army camped
on this same half of the South. Corn and
what little wheat could then be grown,
with rice and sorghum syrup, formed the
base of our supplies. Of course fruits and
vegetables were grown, but being perish-
able were worthless for our soldiers or prisoners, so limited were our means of trans-
portation.

Northern journals often ask why it was
that the South gave Northern prisoners
nothing to eat ; and I must say here, that
there is a sorrow deep-felt at the knowl-
edge that our soldiers and the Northern
prisoners both suffered for the want of
sufficient food to nourish ; they suffered
both as to quantity and quality. But I ask
in all candor, how could it be otherwise,
hemmed in as the South was ? Not one
tenth of the government tithes of grain

and meat, west of the Mississippi River, could reach us ; the blockade was all around; the Federal army's tents were pitched on Southern soil ; detachments of the Union army were invading the narrowing space of territory left to raise provisions on, and were decoying off the laborers and destroying and laying waste the country through which they marched ; every means we had to feed either our army or the Northern prisoners was disabled.

My brothers wrote home (without murmur or discontent) that they were living the greater part of the time on parched corn, which they either bought or begged ; that they were foraging around in the country, on the mountain sides, and in the valleys, for succulent roots, leaves, and berries to allay the pangs of hunger ; sassafras bushes were stripped in a trice of leaves, twigs, and bark, and eaten' ravenously. They wrote that sometimes for two or three months they never saw so much as a slice of bacon, and then perhaps for a week or two a rasher of bacon the size of a pocket-knife would be issued to each man of their regiment. One of my brothers once drew from his pocket, when asked about his slice of bacon, the pocket-knife which he brought home after the war was over, and said : " It is a fact ; the rasher of bacon was no longer, and about just as thick and wide as this knife."

Such a slice they held over the fire with bread underneath to catch the drippings, so as to lose none. A brother-in-law of mine told me that he, as well as other soldiers of his division, lived on parched corn most of the time ; sometimes they had roasting ears, either roasted in the ashes or eaten raw ; that if they had money, they would buy the corn ; if not, beg it ; and at times they would be so crazed with hunger that if neither money nor begging would get it, they would steal it. At first the men were punished for stealing something to eat, but at last the sight of our hollow-eyed and ragged, emaciated soldiers appealed so to the sympathies of the officers that they could not find it in their hearts to punish their men for trying to keep soul and body together with pilfered corn. Times were almost as hard with citizens all over the South the last year of the war, as with our soldiers. Corn was twelve and thirteen dollars per bushel, and our government's pay to its soldiers was only eleven dollars per month; so one whole month's wages would not quite buy a bushel of corn.

What could be grown of provisions, in the waning of our Confederacy, was shared equally and willingly between our soldiers and their Northern prisoners. I verily believe, in the pressing need of the times the prisoners had the greater share. That was little enough, to be sure, but in that narrow space that was left to us as the Northern army advanced, where we had to hold our prisoners, there was almost no food or forage to be had. When the great " book of remembrance " is opened to view, on its pages white and fair the North will surely see, not that the South would not, but that the South could not, better feed the Northern prisoners, with all the mighty pressure that was being brought to bear against us. And of this fact I am very sure that, had there been an exchange of prisoners between the North and South toward the last days of our Confederacy, such as there was at first, and such as the whole South from our chief executive down to the humblest citizen was begging and praying for, as much for the unfortu-

nate prisoners among us, as to have our
soldiers in the ranks of our army again,
there never would have been an Anderson-
ville.

XI.

LEAVING a broken home circle, I returned to southern Alabama, where everything was moving on as before ; the thump
of the house-loom and the whirring of the
spinning - wheel were just as regular in
every household ; substitutes and expedients were still being devised or improved
upon.   There was no diminution of patience or perseverance, and we still felt,
in that section, none of the effects of war,
saving the privations and inconveniences
to which allusion has been made.

We still had our merry social gatherings.   Now and then a homespun wedding
would occur, in which the bride and all
who were bidden would be in homespun
out and out.   We were invited to one such
marriage in our settlement.   I wore a
homespun dress of my own labor, but I
neither carded, spun, nor wove it.   I had
become quite skillful in crocheting capes,
vandykes, shawls, scarfs, and gloves, and

as I had had more than enough work carding and spinning my second homespun
dress, I took a neighbor at her word, when
she said : "I'll give you a hank of thread
to crochet me a cape like yours." The
hank would weave one yard of cloth, and
I could crochet two capes per week, be-
sides discharging my school duties faith-
fully. I thus made two yards of cloth
clear, as the thread was furnished for whatever piece I crocheted. More or less in
cuts of thread were paid, according to the
article I furnished, whether shoulder-cape,
vandyke, shawl, or gloves. At one time I
had so many hanks of homespun thread
that they were quite a weight to lift, and
I was proud of them, too, so proud that
if a neighbor came to spend the afternoon,
I always drew forth that bunch of thread
from the large wardrobe where I kept it
hanging, for her to view. Beside having
enough for another full homespun dress,
and all my knitting and crocheting, I sent
to my mother as many as twenty hanks,
that had been paid me for knitting and
crocheting shawls, capes, vandykes, and
similar articles for neighbors.

I had the thread for the dress just men-

tioned dyed blue with our home-made indigo, and a deep garnet with a strong tea
of pine-tree roots. One-half was dyed blue,
the other half garnet. In the warp it was
four blue, and four garnet threads. Two
shuttles were used, one with a blue quill
of thread, the other with a garnet quill, and
the result was a neat and simple plaid. I
cut the buttons out of a gourd shell, and
covered them with scraps of red merino.
We always took pains to take such buttons
off when our homespuns required washing.
When the stuff had been starched and
ironed, we stitched the buttons on again.

The bride's dress was woven a solid
light gray color, warp and woof ; the buttons were made of gray thread, overcast with white thread. Special pains had
been taken with some white cotton flannel,
three rows of which, about three inches
wide, were placed around the bottom of
the skirt, with about three inches' space
between each row. The cuffs, collar, and
shoulder - cape were trimmed with this
white cotton flannel; and from only across
the room it appeared as if the bride wore a
real fur-trimmed dress, and the effect was
graceful in the extreme.

Thread was often spun, both wool and cotton, with the band crossed, so as to knit and crochet with single thread. The wheel-band was crossed only in twisting thread for sewing or knitting purposes. In spinning the single strand the band was always uncrossed, unless we wanted to knit or crochet something very fine and soft, and did not want it double and twisted. Then it was spun with the band of the wheel crossed, so that in crocheting or knitting it would not become untwisted. The cotton thread was bleached by placing it on a line in the yard, where it hung for two or three weeks in the sun and dew. It was a common thing to see long rows of hanks of cotton thread hanging on a line out in the yards or gardens of all the dwellers of our settlement. Such thread would bleach almost as white as snow.

Now and then the stern fruits of war were forced upon our community by the home-coming of some Confederate soldier seriously or fatally wounded ; or by the arrival of the corpse of some one of our soldiers whom we had seen quit the neighborhood in the flush of health and confident that the demands of the South would soon be allowed.

On one occasion I wept with a widow bereft of her only son and child, who had died in a hospital near Richmond, from wounds received in battle. She told us that when he had left for the front, in the midst of her terrible grief, her last words to him as she held his hand had been, "My son, remember it is just as near heaven in Virginia as it is here in our home in Alabama." Years after the young man had been buried, I happened one Sunday to be attending divine service in Hamilton, Georgia, and in the course of his sermon the Rev. William Boothe, a godly Methodist minister, enforced his text by relating an incident. He told how a young man native of Alabama, wounded in battle, lay dying in a hospital near Richmond. The minister, in visiting that hospital, speaking words of cheer and comfort to the sick, was touched by the sight of the young man, who, it was plain to see, was in immediate danger of death. Taking the hand of the dying boy, Mr. Boothe had said in a kindly, fatherly way, "My son, is there any message or word you would like me to send, or, perhaps, that I can bear myself to your people, wherever they may

live ?" A glad smile lighted up the pale
face of the soldier, who quickly replied,
"I am so thankful that some kind friend
will bear a message to my mother, who is
a widow living down in Alabama. I am
her only son and child. Please say to her
from me these words : ' Remember that it
is just as near heaven in Virginia as it is
in our home in Alabama.' There has never
been a night on the tented field, or when
entering into battle, when those words, my
mother's words, and spoken as I left her,
have not been with me." So speaking, the
soldier's face was lighted up by a seraphic
smile, and he expired.

We were fighting hard at home to keep
the upper hand of the difficulties which
hedged us in ; we were working and fasting and praying that victory might reward
all our sacrifices and sufferings, yet day
by day the newspapers brought news of
defeat after defeat ; day by day they told
us of the inexorable advance of the Federal
troops ; day by day the conviction strength-
ened with us that, struggle as we would,
we were on the losing side, and ours was
to go down to history as "the lost cause."
Our soldiers were living on parched corn,

as they had been for a year; they were going into battle ragged and barefoot and half-starved — in vain.

What a fearful day it was for us, when, in April, 1865, word came into our placid valley that the Northern army was almost at our doors! I could not begin to describe our chagrin and terror. In life one is likely to remember always the exact circumstances under which the first shock of bad news was received. I know that the first tidings of the approach of the Yankee forces came to me as I was about to open the gate leading out on to the public road from Mr. G——'s homestead. I was on my way to the school, when a man rode up, and halting an instant said, "General Grierson and his army are marching from Mobile to Eufaula, and they will probably reach Eufaula to-night, or early to-morrow morning!"

As Mr. G—— lived near the main highway, he did not expect to escape the invading army. Now, it seemed, we were to be awakened from the even tenor of our way, perhaps to know another meaning for "hard times." Fear was depicted on every face, for who could tell but that the mor-

row's sun would cast its beams upon a heap
of smoking ruins, and we be bereft of all
the property we had.

Teaching school was not to be thought
of until our suspense was over. The blue
heavens, so vast and serene, seemed no
longer to clasp, mildly and lovingly, our
quiet home in all-embracing arms, nor to
smile upon us in peace and love. " Now,"
thought we, " we shall realize in part, perhaps fully, what ' Old Virginia' and the
Border States have passed through for four
years, while with us, in the blockaded interior, all has been so quiet and undisturbed."

How vividly I remember that day of suspense, as the courier heralded from house
to house his unwelcome message, " The
Yankees are coming !"   The explosion of
a bomb in each one's yard could not have
created greater excitement.   Planters hastily fled to the swamps and the deep, un-
frequented woods, with their stock and
valuables.   At intervals throughout the
day, droves of cattle and hogs were driven
past my employer's residence to hiding-
places in the woods ; and wagons and car-
riages, filled with whatever valuables could

be quickly gotten together, were also passing by.

It was amusing, as well as sad, to see a feather-bed protruding at least a quarter of its length from a carriage window. In our great anxiety, appearances were not regarded. The single thought of the people was to protect themselves and their property as expeditiously and securely as possible. In the mean time we were confused and distracted by conflicting rumors. At one time the report would be, "The army is not a mile off;" then we imagined we heard guns firing. Again it would be, "They are not coming this way at all." Then, "They are only half a mile off," and we were sure we saw the smoke from some burning dwelling or gin-house.

It was a day of unceasing flurry and excitement, and as the lengthening shadows gave warning that night was drawing on, with troubled feelings we looked from face to face, for no one was left to meet the Federal army, should it pass by on our road, save women and children and the negro slaves. Mr. G—— was in a deep swamp, about half a mile from his dwelling, with all the stock and what was most valuable. His presence with us would have done no good, for if the enemy had come, he might have been hung before our eyes ; or he might have been tortured to make him tell where his gold and silver were hidden. Men were so treated in many instances.

There were some comical places thought of in which to hide gold, silver, jewelry, and other valuables. A lady of our settlement wrapped her watch and chain, bracelets, and a valuable breast - pin, together with some other jewelry, in an old faded rag, and tossed it into the middle of a large rose-bush in her front yard. There it remained secure, although the house and yard were filled with Yankee soldiers, who searched the house, turning up beds and mattresses, pulling the clothing out of the wardrobe and bureaus ; and yet that rose-bush kept its secret.

Another young woman took her father's bag of gold and silver, and ran to the hen-house and put it beneath the nest of a setting hen. An old lady put all her jewelry in a small jar, cemented the top tightly on, placed it in an old bucket, and let it down into her well. When all things had settled down quietly, and it was safe to draw the jar from the well, nothing was found to be soiled or injured in the least. Another filled an old ash-hopper with bacon, covered it with a cloth, put ashes over that about half a foot deep, then with straw built a hen's nest or two, and placed some eggs in them; and of course the Yankee soldiers cared nothing for that insignificant ash-hopper and its hen's nest.

As darkness closed in, we sat with folded hands and bated breath, listening for the tramp of the mighty Northern host, with the unexpressed thought, "Woe is me, that I sojourn in Mesech, that I dwell in the tents of Kedar!" In the midst of silent reveries around the fire, for the night was chill, and a fire had been kindled, in part to dispel the gloom and dread of our feelings, one of the daughters turned to her cousin and said, "Annie, what will you do if the Yankees come?" "Ooo-oo-o!" with hands upraised, was the reply. Then cousin Annie turned to her cousin, after a long pause, and asked, "Marie, what will you do if they come?" "Umph-mph-ph," with eyes dilated, was Marie's reply. Never a word was spoken save that question, followed by an inarticulate exclamation. Finally it seemed so ludicrous that we all broke forth into merry peals of laughter, which served as a safety-valve to our genuine depression.

A married daughter of Mr. G——'s was living in a small cottage near her father's, built so that he might have his daughter under his care while her husband was away in our army. The married daughter did not feel disposed to leave her house exposed, but was too much alarmed to remain alone that night with her two small children. So she urged me to stay with her, as her mother would have the cousin and two older daughters. As I was going down the colonnade steps, with the two young girls, aged between nine and eleven, Mrs. G—— called to me, "Miss A——, if the Yankees come, I shall be sure to send Martha (the colored nurse girl) to tell you." "All right," I replied, "you'll see how fast I shall get to you."

In painful apprehension we sat long on the porch. It was one of those half-moonlit nights, so calm that the stillness was oppressive. But exhausted nature demanded her tribute, and finally we sought rest from

the day's worry and suspense in sleep, un-
easy though it might be. God only knows
how fervent and plaintive was the prayer
that ascended that April night in southern
Alabama, from hundreds of dwellings peopled only by women, children, and negro
slaves. As I pillowed my head, I called up
soul-comforting passages from the Bible,
none bringing greater solace than, " The
angel of the Lord encampeth round about
them that fear Him." The ninety-first
Psalm, that I had committed to memory
in Sabbath-school, now came to mind like
a great wave of consolation.

I was just bordering upon the edge of
sleep, when I was suddenly startled by a
loud and hurried knocking on the door,
and immediately recognized the voice of
the negro girl, who was excitedly crying
out, " Miss A——, missis say come down
dar quick, de Yankees coming." I sprang
with a sudden bound into the middle of
the room, gathered up shoes and stockings
in one hand, dress and other garments in
the other, and dashed out in the shadowy
night, with the two little girls, who had just
as hastily left their bed, and now clung
on either side of me in their long white

night-robes. A dark cloud skurried across
the moon and obscured its light for a moment, making the night darkish, but in
another instant all the clouds had rolled
by, and left the moon clear, so that the
shadows of the great oaks were distinctly
outlined, quivering beneath our feet as we
flew past. One of the little girls tripped,
but managed to gather herself up quickly,
without ever letting go of me, to whom
she clung with the grip of the Old Man of
the Sea.

As we reached the side entrance of the
main yard, and passed through the gate,
we found the yard swarming with the
negro slaves; passing the kitchen, which
was detached from the main dwelling-
house (as at all Southern homes in those
days), Uncle Ben and Aunt Phillis were
standing in the doorway. They craned
their necks, shaded their eyes with their
hands, and peered forth at us in the darkness, as we passed swiftly by. " Well
I 'clare fore God " — The rest of the
sentence was lost in our hurried flight.
We jammed against Aunt Jemimah, the
regular washerwoman, who held in her
hands a pair of cotton-cards, and on whose

arm was hanging a wisp of white cotton rolls. She threw up her arms at sight of us, the wisp of rolls floating lightly away on the night breeze. When she recognized us, she exclaimed, " Lors, chilluns, I did just tink you was ghosses."

We entered the house by the back door, just in time to find all in great confusion, caused by a false alarm. The home guards, composed of old men and young boys of the county, had that afternoon disbanded in the city of Eufaula, knowing that General Grierson would arrive that night or the next morning, and that resistance would be useless. So they deemed discretion just then the better part of valor, and here they were, returning home by the road on which my employer's plantation lay, their expectation being that the Federal commander would march his column into Eufaula by a road on the other side of our settlement.

When the horses' hoofs struck the bridge that spanned a large creek, three or four hundred yards from Mr. G——'s mansion, the sounds, borne on the still night air with startling distinctness, were naturally mistaken by lone women and chil-

dren for the advance of the terrible Yankees. When the Babel-like confusion had
ceased we presented a droll tableau, for,
acting on the impulse of the moment, no
one had paused to think of personal appearance.

When asked what she was going to do
with the cotton-cards and wisp of rolls,
Aunt Jemimah's reply was, "Oh, lor bless
yer, honeys, I did n't know I had 'em." It
had been usual to allow the negroes the
use of the wheels and cotton-cards, and
cotton was given them, in case they wished
to spin their own stocking-yarn or sewing-
thread at night.

The negroes, too, had been expecting
the Yankee army, and hearing a great
clashing of horses' hoofs on the bridge,
thought with the rest of us, " They are
coming now." So large and small left the
" quarter " and came over to " Marster's,"
as they called the dwelling-house and yard,
to see the Federal troops. Perhaps some
may have come with the design of going
with the Yankees. The cottage of the
married daughter and the negroes' quarter
were about equally distant from my employer's residence, but in opposite direc-

tions, so that by the time I had reached the yard of the dwelling, I found myself in a surging mass of black humanity.

In calling to mind the scenes of that night, I have often thought that had the Federal army really come, and the two little girls and I dashed into view in our long white robes, fleeing as if on the wings of the wind, we should have caused the moving host to halt. And oft as memory recalls those scenes I rub my eyes and ask, "Can it be that on that long April night in 1865, while the Federal army was marching into Eufaula by another road, we women and children, surrounded by negro slaves, were the sole occupants of that exposed house?" Yet so in truth it was. We felt no fear of the slaves. The idea of any harm happening through them never for one instant entered our minds.

But now, not for my right hand would I be situated as I was that April night of 1865. Now it would by no means be safe, for experience is showing us that in any section where the negro forms any very great part of the population, white men or women are in danger of murder, robbery, and violence.

XII.

WHEN the morning came after that miserable night, another courier passed through our settlement, ending our state of uncertainty with the information that the Northern army was in Eufaula. We had been entirely passed by, after all our tumult and apprehension. How thankful we were, Heaven only knows!

Mr. G—— came in towards night with all his stock, saying he hoped he should never have to spend another night in that uncanny dark swamp, with its tall trees all festooned with gray moss, almost reaching to the ground, and swaying to and fro, as a shiver of moaning wind would stir the air. The hooting of owls, and croaking of frogs would sound at intervals, the unrest and stamping of the tied-up stock, together with the terrible suspense of how it would fare with his family and his belongings, if the opposing army should pass his plantation, made it anything but pleasant, it may well be imagined.

Yet in our great rejoicing that we had been passed by, our hearts went out in sympathy to our less fortunate neighbors, many of whom were despoiled of everything valuable. I knew families that were bereft of everything; who had not so much left as would furnish one meal of victuals; whose dwelling-houses, gin-houses, and bales of cotton were all left in smoking ruin. In many instances women and children would have to stand by helpless, and see their trunks, bureaus, and wardrobes kicked open. Whatever struck the soldier's fancy was appropriated; to the rest of the contents, as apt as not, a match would be applied, and the labor of years would swirl up in smoke.

Amid this pillage and plunder, some absurd incidents now and then occurred, one or two of which I will mention.

Many of the planters, large and small, had turned their attention to stock-raising, among other industries needful and enforced by the blockade. One man said, as bacon was so scarce and high priced, he was going to raise a herd of goats to help along. He got a few to begin with, and as he had a good range of piney woods for them to graze in, he soon had a fine herd. These the invading army passed by as utterly unworthy of their attention.

When the war closed there were some fine young colts, two and three years old, coming on in the South. A planter who lived near us had several, which I remember were named after Lee, " Stonewall " Jackson, and other popular leaders. This planter was very fond of his young daughter, who usually accompanied him when he walked out to his pasture-lot. He used to say to the little girl, when admiring his young colts, " These are papa's fine stock." When the Federal army came, it so happened that this planter got the news only in time to be just disappearing down a hill near his house, with all his horses and mules, as the Yankees approached ; his young colts being left in their pasture. Finding no stock in the lot or outbuildings, the soldiers threatened to shoot a little negro boy who was in the yard, if he did not tell them where the stock were hidden. Hearing the threat, the planter's daughter said, in the innocence of her heart, " Papa's fine stock is over there," pointing to the field where the young colts were grazing.

Away dashed the soldiers, sure of a rich prize. Meantime the planter had had time to flee with his stock to a secure hiding-place, chosen for the occasion which had now arrived.

Great was the surprise of the soldiers, after making a sweep of the field, to find only a few small colts quietly feeding, unmindful that they were " papa's fine stock." The soldiers returned furious with disappointment, and played sad havoc with all the buildings, burned the gin-house and barns, ransacked the dwelling from cellar to attic, broke up furniture, and appropriated whatever was valuable that could be easily carried with them. It really seemed as if the wreck was a greater blow than the loss of the stock would have been, and for a few days there was sore grief in that household. But they soon roused themselves, on reflection that they yet had their stock left to plow the already planted crop, and a roof over their heads, while many were left without stock to tend their crop, or house to rest in.

A disabled soldier of our Confederacy, who lived in the southern part of Alabama, near the Choctawhatchee River, with his wife and five small children was visiting relatives in our neighborhood. They had driven through in their own carriage, to which two fine horses were hitched. They had packed in their carriage what was most useful and valuable to them as wearing apparel, all their valuables in jewelry and plate, bed-quilts, counterpanes, a feather-bed and pillows, bandboxes, hatboxes, trunks, and many other articles of value. I saw the carriage unpacked, and stood amazed that such a quantity of stuff could be stowed in such a small space. They had been careful to take all the best belongings of their house, because it was expected that the Federal army would come directly through their settlement, as they were not far from Mobile, and on the route to Eufaula. In our neighborhood, it was not believed at first that the enemy would find us, hence they left their own home to visit the relatives who lived near us. But rumors began to fly thick and fast when it was known positively that General Grierson was on the march from Mobile, and then it was believed that he would surely come by on our road.

So the disabled Confederate soldier and his family packed their carriage again, and left our settlement. They made for the public road which, according to their theory, would be the one General Grierson would be least likely to choose to march into Eufaula by. They proceeded seven or eight miles undisturbed by anything, and were congratulating themselves on being so fortunate as to flank the enemy, when just as they turned a bend of the road that led into another, alack-a-day! there was one moving mass of "blue," up the road and down the road, as far as the eye could see.

They had driven altogether unexpectedly right into the midst of the Yankee soldiers. I am sorry to say they were called to a halt immediately; their horses were cut (not unhitched) from the carriage. The wife begged to be spared the horses, but finding pleading of no avail, she let loose her tongue in such a way that one of the soldiers raised his gun and threatened to shoot her if she did not keep quiet. She stood fair and fearless, and told him to shoot. He was not so heartless, however, as to put his threat into execution. Noth-

ing was taken, except the horses. The
wife and children had to remain in the
open pine barrens, while the husband
walked several miles before he could get
assistance to drag the carriage to the nearest house. And after all, when this man
reached his own home again, he found that
it had not been molested, inasmuch as the
Federal army had passed him by, by several miles. But one could never tell, in
the midst of innumerable conflicting asser-
tions, what it was best to do.

About six months before General Robert
E. Lee's surrender, business called Mr.
G—— to Columbus, Georgia, and while
there he found a gentleman so embar-
rassed by debt that he was forced to sell
some of his slaves. Mr. G—— bought
two young negro men, Jerry and Miner by
name, paying six thousand five hundred
dollars apiece for them. Mr. G—— would
always look on the bright side, and would
never give in to the idea that the South
would, or could, be conquered, — high-
toned, generous old Virginia gentleman
that he was! What a laugh we all had
when he came home and said, " Well, I 've
got two negroes now, who must be good

for something if the price has anything to
do with them ; I've paid thirteen thousand
for two young negro boys." His amiable
and gentle wife rebuked him for his indis-
cretion in buying negroes at that time, as
we believed that they would soon have
an opportunity of leaving, if they chose to
do so. But he pooh-poohed her, saying,
"Wait till you get to the bridge before you
cross the river."

In a very short time the surrender came ;
the South was overrun by Federal soldiers ;
and I smile even now, when I recall one
morning at breakfast, when Aunt Phillis
came in from the kitchen to the dining-
room, with a waiter of hot biscuits just
from the oven, — for no one thought of
finishing breakfast without a relay of hot
biscuits toward the middle or end of the
meal, — and said, as she handed the biscuits round, "Jerry and Miner done gone
back to Columbus !" I marveled much
at Mr. G——'s philosophical remark, as
he paused with cup suspended, "Humph ;
that's the dearest nigger hire I ever paid !
Six thousand five hundred dollars apiece
for six months," sipping his coffee and placing the cup back in the saucer.

I looked at him closely. There was not even the tinge of bitterness in his remark, and I thought, " Here is philosophy that would shame the Stoics." It had not been a twelvemonth back that, when it became necessary for him to leave the plantation for a day only, he had given orders that Jim be well cared for; for if Jim died, he would lose more than a thousand dollars in gold. Now he had lost in all about eighty or one hundred thousand dollars, all gold value, gone like the lightning's flash, — who can doubt but that a kind Providence tempered the resignation with which we met the inevitable?

I remained some years after the war in that settlement, and never a bitter or harsh word, no, not one, did I ever hear my employer utter against the opposing army, or section of States, that had caused all the turn - round of affairs in the South; that, metaphorically speaking, had caused riches to take to themselves wings and fly away.

The same cannot be said of all the people of the South, but it is pleasing to think that all can now recall the history of those days, when the opposing army was marching through the South, leaving a desert waste behind them, without feeling the bitterness we then felt, standing in the midst of our desolation ; and God knows that we give heart and hand in cordial welcome to the soldiers of that Northern host which so despoiled us, as well as to the people of the Northern States when they make choice, as many are now doing, of our sunny clime for their own home.

XIII.

THE return of our soldiers after the surrender, in their worn and ragged gray, as they tramped home by twos, threes, and sometimes in little squads of half a dozen or more, was pitiable in the extreme.

Some were entirely without shoes or hats; others had only an apology for shoes and hats. They were coming home with nothing; and we could almost say, coming home to nothing; for many verily found, when they reached the spot that had been to them a happy home, nothing save a heaped-up mass of ruins left to them. Often as I sit in the twilight and drift back into the past, it is not easy to restrain tears, as memory views those soldiers in their worn gray, marching home sad and depressed, with the cause the had so warmly espoused, lost.

Though not coming rejoicing, as did the Athenians and Spartans from the battle of Platæa, they were just as dear to the hearts of their kindred at their ruined homes, as if they had come marching in triumph, with olive - wreaths encircling their brows.

Need there be wonder if, for a few weeks, it seemed as though we were petrified, — scarcely knowing which way to turn, to restore order out of such chaos ! Another day of fasting and prayer was called in our adversity that our spirits might be tempered to bear the result. But our thoughts soon turned resolutely from the gloomy picture, the more readily when we remembered how the South had met emergencies during the war, until she was so environed and crippled by opposing forces that she *had* to yield. The same energy, perseverance, and economy, with the help of an overruling Providence, would yet make the South smile with peace and plenty.

Our returned soldiers lost no time in making themselves useful in every sphere of honorable work that then opened. Many of those who returned in April planted corn and cotton, late as it was, and made fair crops of both. There was great bother for awhile as to plow stock, for most of

our valuable animals had been carried off
by the invading army.

Three brothers whom I knew, natives of
Georgia, owned not one foot of land nor an
animal of any kind, when the war closed.
They reached home among the first of our
returning soldiers. They rented a good
piece of farming land, managed to get an
ox and an old broken-down army mule, and
set to work in earnest on their rented
land. They "put in" every hour of the
sun, and the greater part of the light of
the moon. Neighboring farmers said that
at whatever hour of the night you passed
where the brothers farmed, if the moon
shone you would hear them "gee-hawing,"
plowing their crop at night, or the clashing of their hoes in their corn, cotton, or
peas. They are now prosperous farmers,
owning broad acres of land and fine stock.
Hundreds of similar cases might be pointed
out.

When our soldiers returned we were always deeply interested in hearing them re-
count, when we met them at social gatherings at some neighbor's house, the straits
to which they were reduced toward the
last days of the war, and on the home

march after the surrender. A brother-in-
law of mine, who became bare as to pants,
and had no way of getting any in his then
distressed state, had recourse to his army
blanket, and having no scissors with which
to cut the blanket, he used his pocket-
knife for that purpose. He sharpened a
stick with his knife to make holes in each
half of the blanket, which he tied up separately with the raveling of the blanket:
making each leg of the pants separately.
They were tied around his waist with a
string. He managed to get on for quite a
while with his blanket pants, but met a
comrade more fortunate than the rest of
the soldiers of our cause, in that, beside
having a passable pair of pants, he had
rolled up under his arm a half worn osnaburg pair of pants, also. These my
brother-in-law bought of him for four hundred dollars. He wore them home after
the surrender, and that same half-worn,
four-hundred-dollar pair of osnaburg pants
did service for some time on the farm after the war.

When one of my brothers, who was
taken prisoner at Appomattox during the
last days of fighting in Virginia, and who

was sent to Point Lookout in Maryland, was paroled with many others, and sent by steamer to Savannah, Georgia, he and they had to "foot it" the greater part of the way to Columbus, Georgia, where most of them lived, inasmuch as the Federal army had torn up the railroads and burnt all the bridges. They were all more or less lacking as to clothing, but one of the comrade's clothing was in such bad plight that he could scarcely make a decent appearance on the road, much less appear in his own settlement. As they were nearing Columbus, they stopped and advised together as how to overcome the deficiency in their comrade's wardrobe. One of the soldiers happened to have a silver dime (a thing quite rare in those days), which he gave his needy comrade to buy a pair of pants with. They had the good luck to get a half worn pair of jeans pants at a small farm-house in the piney-woods, for the ten cents, and these the soldier wore home.

Five or six years after the war, these two comrades, the one who had given the silver dime and the one who had bought the pants with it, met in Columbus, Georgia. They had been together in camp, in prison, and on that long walk home from Savannah to Columbus, through the grand stretches of piney-woods, covered with the green luxuriant wire-grass of southwestern Georgia, and they recognized each other immediately. One drew from his pocket a crisp five-dollar bill and handed it to the giver of the silver piece, saying, "Take this, old fellow, in grateful acknowledgment for that silver dime I bought those pants with ; for I might almost say, 'I was naked and ye clothed me.'"

XIV.

JUST as soon as the railroads could be repaired and bridges builded anew, I made haste to get to my father's again to find how all had gone with them while our foes were marching through Georgia. I had tried for three months or more to get a letter or message of some sort to them, as they had to me, but all communication for the time being was completely broken up. I had spent many sad hours thinking of those at home, and was almost afraid to hear from them ; but as soon as a train ran to Columbus, I ventured forth.

I had traveled over the same road time and again, on my way to and from home, but now as I beheld the ruins of grim-visaged war, whichever way I cast my eyes, I must confess to a somewhat rebellious and bitter feeling. There are moments in the experience of every human being when the heart overflows like the great Egyptian river, and cannot be restrained. "O thou

great God of Israel !" I cried, " why hast
thou permitted this dire calamity to befall
us ? Why is it that our homes are so despoiled ? " And I marveled not at the
captive Hebrews' mournful plaint, as by
the rivers of Babylon they hung their
harps on the willows.

As the train slowed up on the Alabama side of the Chattahoochee River, I
looked eagerly over to the opposite bank,
where the home of my father was situated.
For a few seconds my pulse must have
ceased to throb, as I beheld the ruins of
the city of Columbus. With others I
took my seat in an omnibus and was
driven to the river's edge, there to await
the coming of the ferry-boat which had
been built since all the bridges on the river
had been burned by the hostile army.
The scene seemed so unreal that like
Abou Hassan, the caliph of fiction, I was
thinking of biting my fingers to make sure
I was really awake. Had I not had my
coin in my hand to pay the ferryman, I
should have imagined we were all shades,
flitting about on the shore of the Styx !

In musing silence, I could but say, O
swift-flowing Chattahoochee, is it thus I

behold thee ? Thou flowest in almost pris-
tine loveliness. Where are your huge
bridges, that linked the green hills of Alabama with the beautiful city of cottages
and flowers ? Where are the cotton mills
and machine-shops that lined your banks,
— mills which from early morn until the
sun set sent forth an incessant hum ? Is it
thus that I behold thee, city of my fathers ?

My reverie was broken when the ferry-
boat reached her landing ; but things all
still seemed so strange that I could scarcely
believe I was not dreaming. I realized
everything better when I saw soldiers in
blue moving hither and thither. I had
heard while on the train, how General
Willson had ravaged, pillaged, and burnt, as
he passed through Alabama. Here were
his soldiers who had laid Columbus in
ruins ; here were they of whom I had been
told that their route from Columbus to the
city of Macon, one hundred miles, could be
plainly traced by the curling smoke arising
from burning dwellings, gin-houses, barns,
bridges, and railroad ties.

I was not long in getting to my father's
after I had left the city of Columbus. And
there was a joyous surprise in every re-

spect, for nothing had been disturbed at
his residence save some corn, fodder, and
other food, which had been appropriated
by raiding soldiers. I found both of my
brothers home. The one who had been
carried to Point Lookout had arrived only
two days before. The one who had been
taken prisoner about three months before
the surrender managed to make his escape the night following the day he was
captured. It was a dark, sleety night,
my brother said, and he had found it quite
easy to elude the sentinel. First he went,
as he supposed, about a mile from the
camp; then he lay down on the frozen
ground with his army blanket, not daring
to light a fire, for fear of recapture. When
the sun rose he took his bearings, and
began his long tramp for home. This
journey had occupied many weeks, as all
traveling had to be done at night, and
often he was in imminent danger of being
recaptured, as the whole country through
which he was passing was filled with Federal cavalrymen. Creeks and rivers had
to be waded or swum ; deep and almost
impenetrable swamps had to be passed.
Once in the thick woods he had come near

running into what he supposed to be a deserters' camp, from the surroundings he descried by the pale glare of the pine-knot camp-fire, but what really was a camp of Northern soldiers. He subsisted on roots and leaves, sometimes calling at a house after dark to beg a few ears of corn, which he parched and ate; sometimes he enjoyed a rare dessert in the berries of the hawthorn bush.

One blustering March night, just as the clock had told the hour of two, the watch-dog at my father's was heard baying furiously at the front gate. There was some one at the gate speaking to the dog, as if trying to quiet him. My father arose, opened the door, and when he could make his voice heard, he called out, "What's wanting?" "It's N——, 'Drive' (the dog's name) won't let me come in." At the name "N——," our mother sprang from the bed with a loud and joyful shout that he who had been mourned as dead was alive and home again. My sisters, who were sleeping up-stairs, were also aroused by the furious barking of the dog. They arose and raised the window-sash just in time to hear, "It's N——." Their window dropped like a flash of lightning, and then such a getting down-stairs as there was! One or two chairs were knocked over in the scramble for the head of the staircase, and one toppled the whole flight of steps, making a great racket, in the middle of the night, as it thumped the steps one by one. The candle, which some one had managed to light while the sash was being raised, was let fall when about in the middle of the flight of steps, and in the then utter darkness one of my sisters stumbled over the chair that had preceded her to the bottom of the stairs, and all came pell-mell into the dark hall. My brother told me afterward that he could not move for some time, he was so tightly pinioned when finally taken to his mother's heart.

What a change from 1861, when all were so buoyant and full of fiery patriotism, with never a thought of being overcome! Now our cause was lost, all our homes more or less despoiled, the whole South seemingly almost hopelessly ruined, every little town and village garrisoned by the troops who had overcome us by great odds.

Yet after all our great and sore afflic-

tions, I found only cheerfulness and Chris
tian resignation at the end of these troublous war times, and the hope that we might
yet rise above our misfortunes.

In closing, I must say that I know that
the people of the Southern States are now
loyal to the Union ; their reverence for
the stars and stripes is strong and pure ;
and it pierces like a sword, our ever being
taunted and distrusted.   Accepting all the
decisions of the war, we have built and
planted anew amid the ruins left by the
army who were the conquerors.   We are
still poor ; but we believe firmly that in
our new life, under God, we are destined
to a brilliant career of prosperity and
glory.   Come, happy day !